THE
POCKET
SURREALISM

Published in 2025
by Gemini Gift Books
Part of Gemini Books Group

Based in Woodbridge and London

Marine House, Tide Mill Way,
Woodbridge, Suffolk IP12 1AP
United Kingdom

www.geminibooks.com

Text and Design © 2025 Gemini Books Group
Part of the Gemini Pockets series

Cover illustration by Natalie Foss

ISBN 978-1-80247-310-0

Manufacturer's EU Representative: Eurolink Compliance Limited, 25 Herbert
Place, Dublin, D02 AY86, Republic of Ireland. admin@eurolink-europe.ie

Printed in China

10 9 8 7 6 5 4 3 2 1

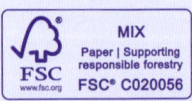

Picture credits: Alamy Stock Photo: Imago: p116; SJArt: p4; The History
Collection: p72. © Archivo Privado de Fotografía y Gráfica Kati y José Horna,
Mexico City: p92. Freepik: p6–7, 10–13, 15–19, 67–8, 70–1, 98–9,103; BRGFX:
p84–5, 87–8, 90–1, 94–7, 100–1; PCH.VECTOR: p118–27; Rawpixel: p22–4, 26–9,
106–7, 110–11; soepratman: p32–8, 40–1; TOHAMINA: p108–9, 112–15; vectorcorp:
p54–61. Getty Images: Archive Photos / Stringer: p62; Keystone Features
/ Stringer: p8; Keystone-France / Contributor: p20, p52; Michael Ochs
Archives / Stringer: p30, p82, p104; Robert Stiggins / Stringer: p42. Noun
Project/Simon Child: p86, 89.

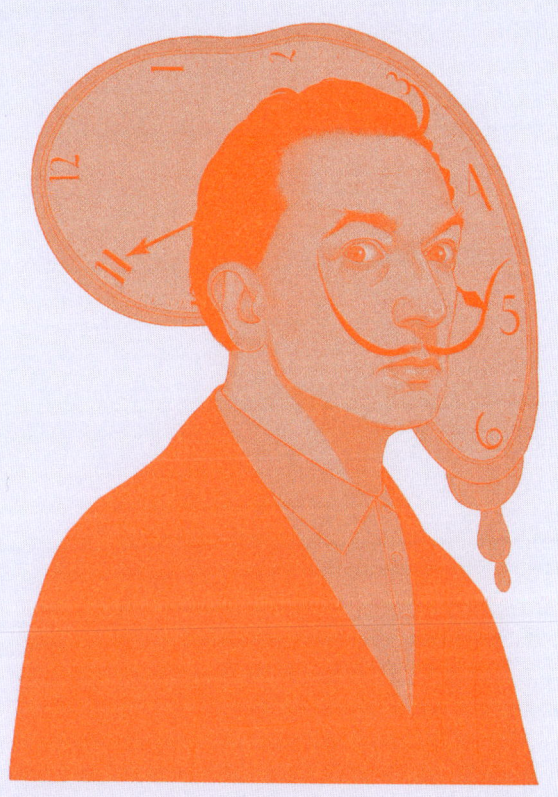

SURREALISM

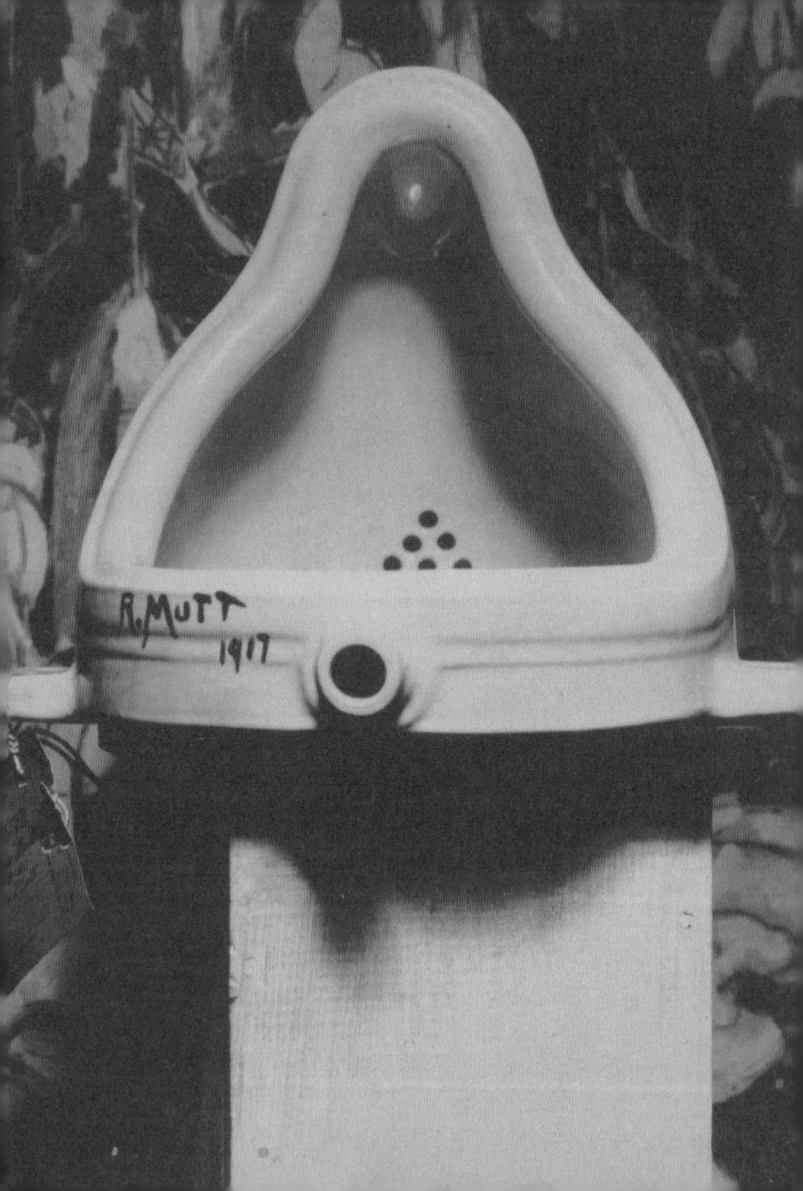

CONTENTS

INTRODUCTION

Dalí's melting clock. Magritte's apple for a face. Photorealism. Intricate scrawling. Dream-like landscapes. Surrealism is a fantastic, hugely popular artform. This book provides an introduction to this beautiful, fascinating and mysterious artistic genre, which made its way into the mainstream from the streets of Paris more than a century ago.

Ten artists have been chosen to demonstrate the breadth, beauty and sheer variety of surrealism for this book. From Dalí and Magritte – the most famous – to the lesser known, but no less important, artists such as Carrington and Varo. While some embraced the label ("I am surrealism," Dalí once famously exclaimed), others did not; but certainly all those selected have contributed to the evolution of this thought-provoking and celebrated movement.

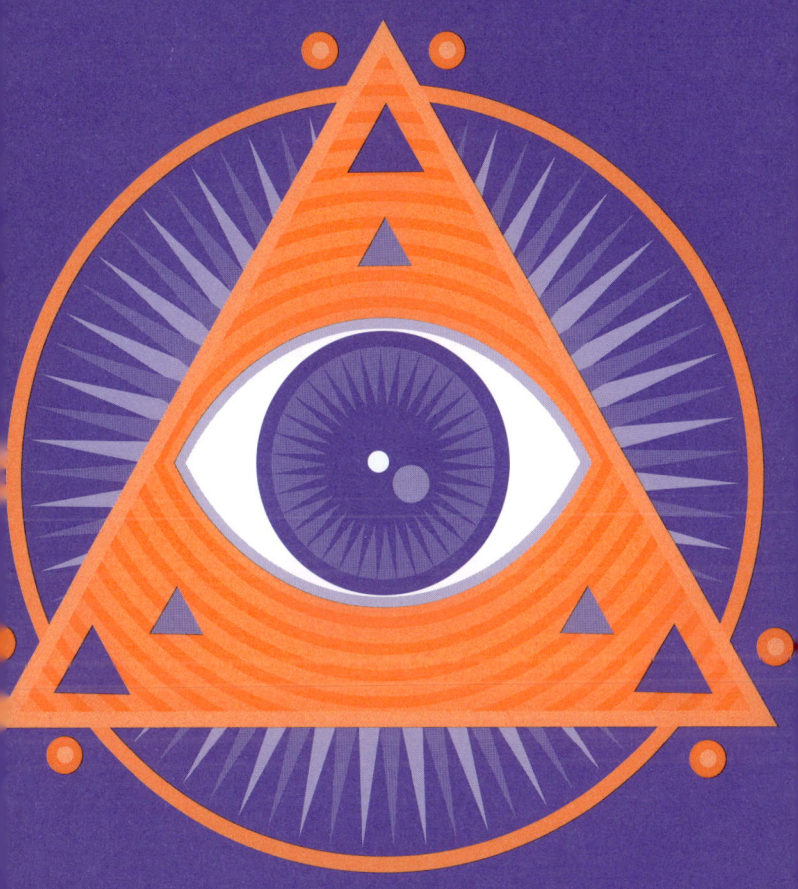

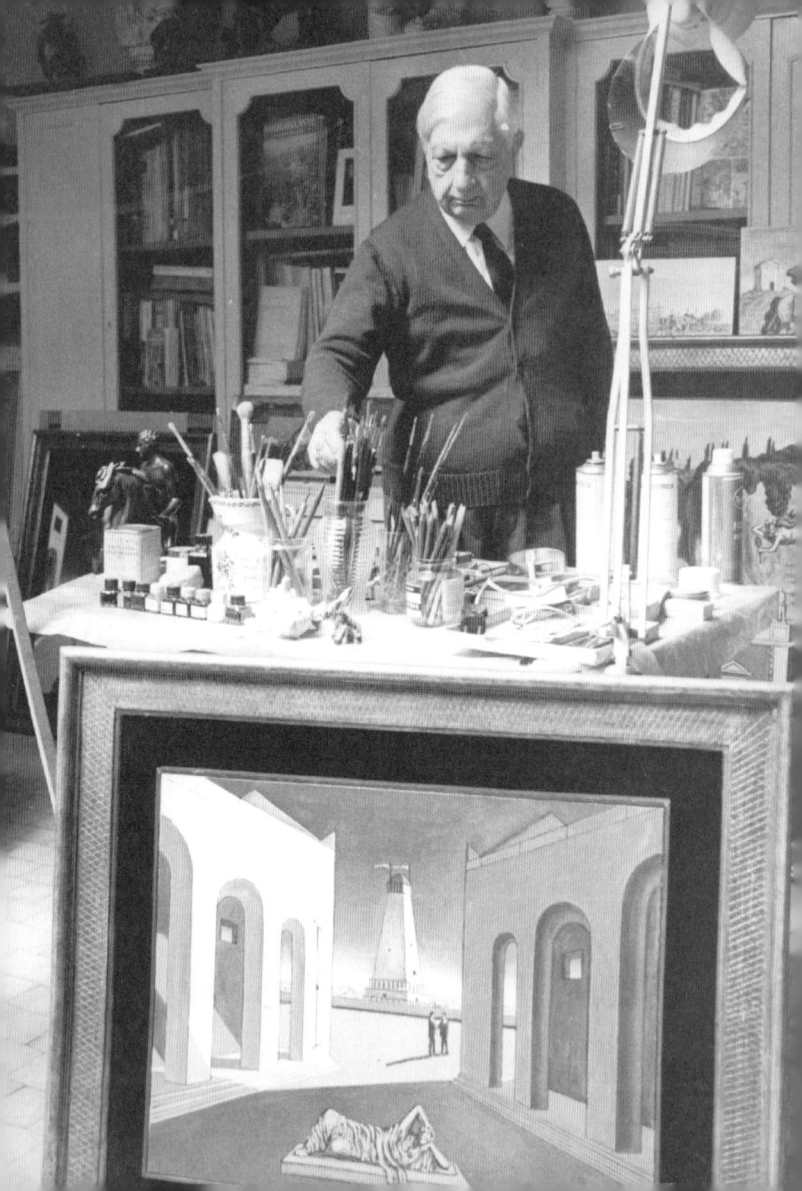

ORIGINS & INFLUENCES

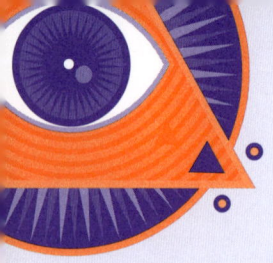
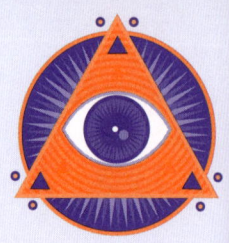

WHAT IS SURREALISM?

It was the French poet Guillaume Apollinaire who first used the term "surrealist" – in 1917. A few years later, in 1924, André Breton, the leader of a group of writers and artists, published the *Manifesto of Surrealism*, which outlined what this intellectual movement was all about.

At that point – just after World War I – the group included writers, poets, artists and all sorts of performers, but the art form we recognize and refer to today as Surrealism is mostly visual.

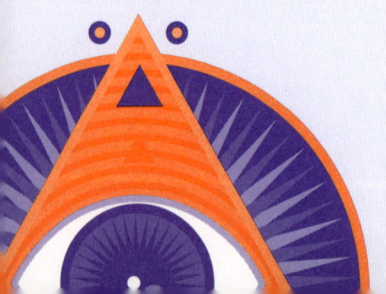
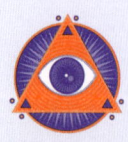

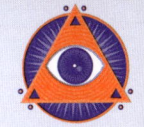

"[Surrealism is] pure psychic automatism, by which one proposes to express, either verbally, in writing, or by any other manner, the real functioning of thought."

ANDRÉ BRETON,
MANIFESTO OF SURREALISM,
1924

ORIGINS

After World War I, France was a hotbed of political and artistic ideas, influence and change. The Dada movement, a direct precursor to Surrealism, was created at this time, challenging the Establishment, rational thought and "bourgeois values", and Marcel Duchamp's *Fountain* (1917) was a key influence (see page 4). By the 1920s, two Surrealist groups had emerged in Paris, but it was the one led by André Breton that became well-known, paving the way for many key artists, including Max Ernst, Salvador Dalí, Man Ray, Joan Miró and Yves Tanguy.

EARLY INFLUENCES

Paintings by Giorgio de Chirico (see page 8) in the 1910s are some of the earliest forms of Surrealism, although the artist abandoned this style soon afterward. Examples include *The Nostalgia of the Infinite* (1912–13) and *The Double Dream of Spring* (1915).

HARLEQUIN'S CARNIVAL

BY JOAN MIRÓ, 1924–25

Location: Buffalo AKG Art Museum, New York, USA

Before he went further into abstract imagery, Joan Miró was one of the founding fathers of Surrealism. One of Miró's early examples of Surrealism, this busy, colourful, complex and exciting piece is one of the best examples of the genre. Imagination and reality merge, and symbols abound. It is now recognized as being one of the most iconic images of the movement.

CORE PHILOSOPHY

Sigmund Freud, the founder of psychoanalysis, was another major influence on Surrealism. Discussions about free association, the subconscious and the analysis of dreams fed in perfectly to the art that was developing at the time. Freedom of the imagination was key, and Breton wrote in his *Manifesto of Surrealism* about the power of "a juxtaposition of two more or less distant realities. The more the relationship between the two juxtaposed realities is distant and true, the stronger the image will be – the greater its emotional power and poetic reality."

RECURRING THEMES

Although by its very nature Surrealist art can really be about anything (as opposed to, say, recognizable objects, a known landscape or an impression of something), there are recurring themes. For example, Salvador Dalí frequently included clocks and desert landscapes, Max Ernst had an obsession with birds and René Magritte combined realistic backgrounds with illusions and incongruous objects. In spite of this, it is one of the most recognizable art forms, and you know a Surrealist image when you see one, whoever the artist and whatever the subject.

"Drawing is the honesty of the art. There is no possibility of cheating. It is either good or bad."

SALVADORE DALÍ
PEOPLE, 1976

A QUESTION OF STYLE

Some artists employed a hyper-realistic style, whereas others used collage, doodles and other non-painting techniques. Sometimes, multiple styles were combined. Surrealist photography, writing and film was also popular.

The original group petered out in the 1940s, but its impact was felt beyond the genre in other movements, such as Abstract Expressionism, and it played a key role in the development of modern art around the world. Today, it has popular appeal, and many artists continue to work under its influence.

"Art has nothing
to do with taste,
art is not there
to be 'tasted'."

MAX ERNST
MAX ERNST: SCULPTURES, 1996

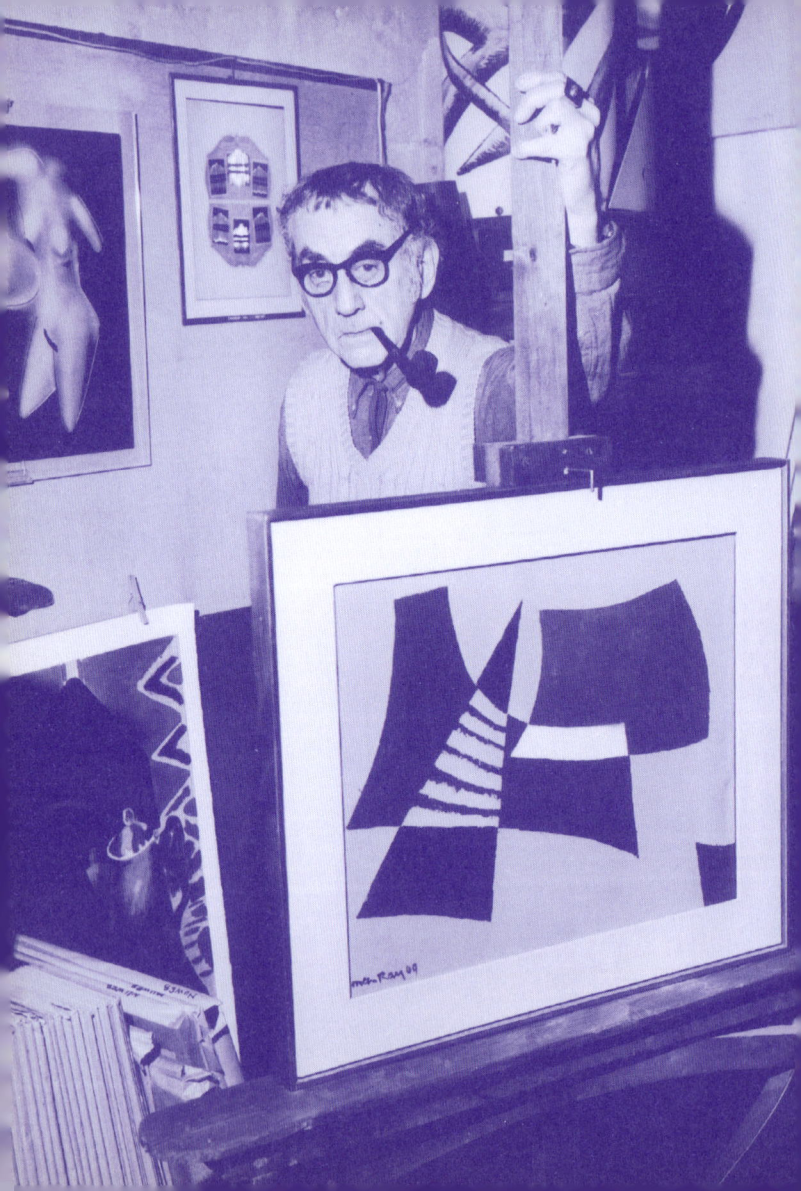

MAN RAY

1890–1976

Place of birth/death:

Pennsylvania, USA/Paris, France

Key works:

L'Enigme d'Isidore Ducasse (The Engima of Isidore Ducasse) (1920)
Objet à détruire (Object to be Destroyed) (1923)
Le Violon d'Ingres (The Violin of Ingres) (1924)
Les Larmes (Glass Tears) (1932)
A l'heure de l'observatoire: Les Amoreux (Observatory Time: The Lovers) (1936)

EARLY YEARS

Man Ray was born Emmanuel Rudnitzky in the USA, the son of Jewish immigrants from Russia. He showed signs of artistic ability from an early age, and began to study art as soon as he finished high school.

In 1915, he met the French artist Marcel Duchamp, and the two worked closely together. They both became important in the Dada movement that was evolving at that time.

"Everything
I do has a
sense, has
a meaning."

MAN RAY,
INTERVIEW WITH
KEITH DEWHURST, FROM THE TV SERIES
REVIEW: ARTISTS AND THEIR ART, 1972

"I seem
to have
become
a legend."

MAN RAY,
PASTDAILY.COM, 1970

FASHION IN FRANCE

In 1921, Man Ray moved to Paris, France. He continued to paint, but also developed a career as a fashion photographer, and was even taking photographs for *Vogue*. One famous work from this era is his photograph *Le Violon d'Ingres*, where the back of a woman (Kiki de Montparnasse) appears to have the f-holes of a musical instrument. It became the most expensive photograph ever sold in 2022, fetching $12 million (£9.5 million).

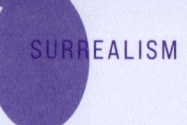

PHOTOGRAPHY AND PAINTING

Between the wars, Man Ray stayed in France, and he took many portrait photographs of famous figures in the art world at that time, including Peggy Guggenheim, Pablo Picasso, Jean Cocteau and Salvador Dalí. He also made movies.

Man Ray returned to the USA during World War II, where he focused on his painting. He stayed there until 1951, when he moved back to Paris. He continued to work on photography, painting and collage until his death in 1976.

"An inanimate object is fascinating, a mystery to me because it survives."

MAN RAY, INTERVIEW WITH KEITH DEWHURST, FROM THE TV SERIES *REVIEW: ARTISTS AND THEIR ART*, 1972

STYLE AND LEGACY

Although remembered as a Surrealist artist, much of Man Ray's work branched into other categories, for example Dadaism and photography. It is worth noting that Man Ray was creating surrealist artwork in the early 1920s before the eponymous movement had even been recognized.

LE CADEAU (THE GIFT)

BY MAN RAY, 1921

Location: The Museum of Modern Art, New York, USA

Shortly before Man Ray's first solo exhibition in Paris, he created this piece from existing three-dimensional objects, using an iron and tacks. It is the perfect example of how he would combine existing objects to make new pieces.

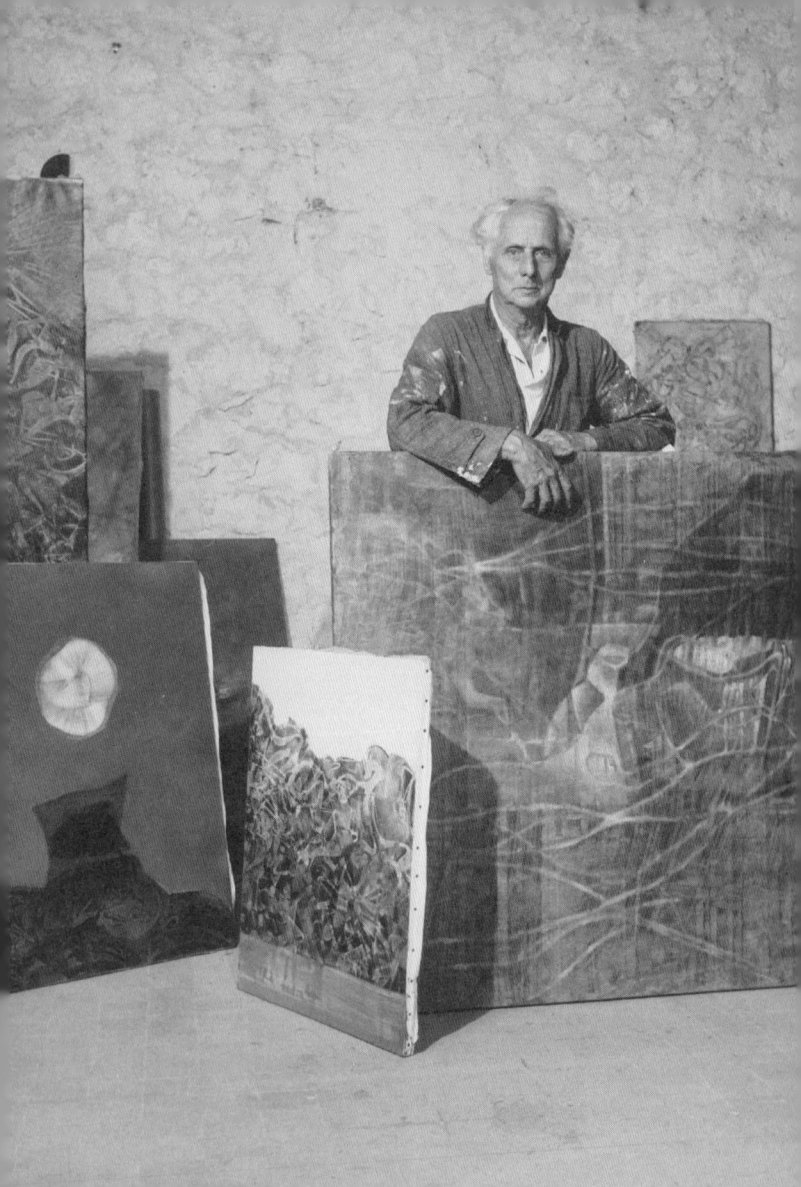

MAX ERNST

1891–1976

Place of birth:

Brühl, Germany/Paris, France

Key works:

The Elephant Celebes (1921)
Ubu Imperator (1923)
Europe after the Rain II (1940–42)
Napoleon in the Wilderness (1941)
The Antipope (1942)

EARLY YEARS

Born near Cologne in Germany in 1891, Max Ernst was one of nine children. His father was a devout Catholic and an amateur painter. Ernst first studied at the University of Bonn, where he read philosophy and art history.

By 1909, Ernst was painting, and his early works were heavily influenced by Picasso, van Gogh and Gaugin. He began exhibiting work as early as 1912.

"Who made art history? Not the most reasonable people, the madmen did."

MAX ERNST,
INTERVIEW WITH
ROLAND PENROSE,
MONITOR, 1961

NEW TECHNIQUES

Ernst served in the military for the whole of the World War I, and was severely affected by the experience. He was able to continue painting, however. By 1919, he had produced some of the collages for which he was later most famous, and at that time he was part of the Dada movement.

In the inter-war years, Ernst spent time in France and worked in "frottage" and "grattage" (techniques he invented), and other original methods of creating art. He left for the USA in 1941, and married Peggy Guggenheim that same year. However, by 1946 he was married to Surrealist artist Dorothea Tanning and settled in California.

"Painting is not for me either decorative amusement, or the plastic invention of felt reality; it must be every time: invention, discovery, revelation."

MAX ERNST,
BEYOND PAINTING, 1937

LATER YEARS

From the 1950s onward, Ernst lived mostly in France, where he continued to paint. In 1954, he won the Grand Prize for Painting at the Venice Biennale. He died in 1976 in Paris, and is buried there in Père Lachaise cemetery.

THE ELEPHANT CELEBES

BY MAX ERNST, 1921

Location: Tate Modern, London, UK

The Elephant Celebes (or *Celebes*) is instantly recognizable, displaying a dream- (or nightmare-) like effect on the viewer. Inspired by de Chirico, it is an early example of Surrealism, and Ernst's first large picture. Proceeds from the sale of the painting in 1975 were gifted to London's Tate Gallery and used to set up a charity for artists, The Elephant Trust, by Roland Penrose and Lee Miller.

BIRDMAN

Ernst had a lifelong fascination with birds, and they are present in his work throughout his career. He even developed an alter ego named "Loplop, Father Superior of the Birds". Loplop became a common figure in Surrealism, gracing the cover of a book, *Surrealists and Surrealism 1919–39* by Gaëtan Picon.

"Surrealism was concerned with the subconscious and with dream imagery... Max Ernst touches far broader bases than that."

DIANE WALDMAN,
CURATOR OF EXHIBITIONS,
*ROUND AND ABOUT
THE GUGGENHEIM*,
1975

A TRUE ARTIST

Ernst had no formal art training, which is extraordinary given the sheer volume, breadth and quality of his work, which incorporates sculpture as well as prints, collage and illustrations. He originated various forms of art, including "automatism", a sort of visual free association without any form of restraint.

Ernst himself compared painting to the process that a poet undergoes when writing: he was an utterly cerebral artist.

THE KING PLAYING WITH THE QUEEN

BY MAX ERNST, 1944

Location: The Museum of Modern Art, New York, USA

This fascinating sculpture, cast in bronze, combines the two notions of chess and sex. The "playing with" of the title is most likely a reference to Ernst himself (the king) and the woman who would become his wife, Dorothea Tanning (the queen). Ernst frequently used the theme of chess in his artwork.

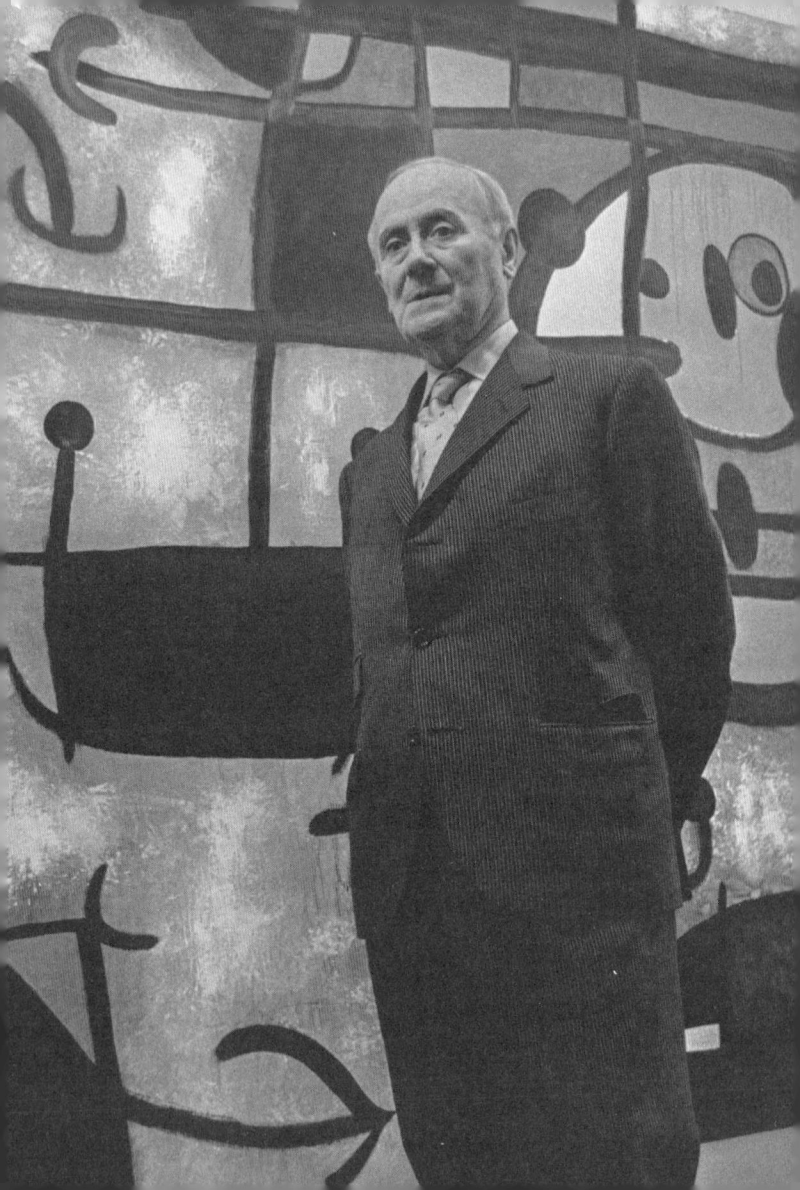

JOAN MIRÓ

1893–1983

Place of birth:

Barcelona, Spain/Palma, Spain

Key works:

The Farm (1921–22)
Harlequin's Carnival (1924–25)
Dutch Interior (I) (1928)
Bleu II (1961)
Woman and Bird (1982)

EARLY YEARS

Joan Miró was born in 1893 in Spain. His father was a watchmaker and his grandfather had been a cabinetmaker. Joan was keen on drawing from a very young age. He first studied art formally in Barcelona, when he was 14, but he was also studying business at the School of Commerce.

His first solo exhibition was held in Barcelona in 1918. However, he did not sell any of his works and the show was panned – even ridiculed – by critics. He headed to Paris in 1920, where he met Pablo Picasso and André Masson.

"By nature, I am tragic and taciturn. In my youth, I endured periods of great sadness."

JOAN MIRÓ,
I WORK LIKE A GARDENER, 1964

STYLISTIC EXPLORATIONS

During the 1920s, Miró divided his time between Paris and his family's farm in Mont-roig del Camp, near Barcelona. In Paris, he had joined up with André Breton's Surrealist group, along with many other artists and writers.

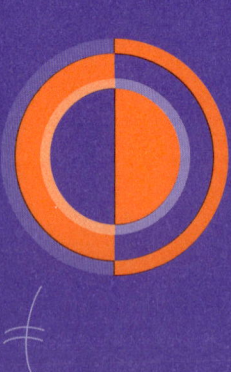

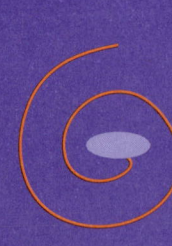

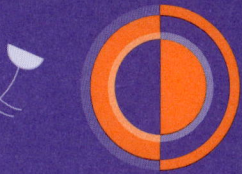

"When I first knew Miró, he had very little money and very little to eat, and he worked all day every day for nine months painting a very large and wonderful picture called *The Farm*."

ERNEST HEMINGWAY ON MIRÓ, 1934

FINDING REFUGE

Throughout the 1930s, Miró was forced to move around, fleeing war in Spain and then in France. He ended up on the island of Mallorca, where he created his famous *Constellations* series (1939–41).

Miró had his first American retrospective exhibition at the Museum of Modern Art in New York in 1941. It was a great success, and after the war his reputation and popularity grew.

"The civil war was all bombings, death, firing squads..."

JOAN MIRÓ,
LETTER TO PIERRE MATISSE,
1940

BEYOND THE SURREAL

From 1954, Miró chose to work only on prints and ceramics, and one of his prominent works from this era included the ceramic murals for the UNESCO building in Paris.

Throughout the 1960s he continued to work prolifically, and was an influence on many other artists and movements, including Pop Art and Abstract Expressionism.

He never stopped creating, and his famous *Woman and Bird* sculpture was unveiled in Barcelona only one year before his death in 1983.

WOMAN AND BIRD

BY JOAN MIRÓ, 1982

Location: Parc de Joan Miró, Barcelona, Spain

One of Barcelona's iconic artistic landmarks, this imposing sculpture covered in brightly coloured broken ceramic tiles, stands 21 metres tall and represents the female with a hat surmounted by a bird. Miró's depiction of birds was a common theme, alluding to their connection between the solid earth and ephemeral sky to reference the world of dreams and our perception of the wider universe.

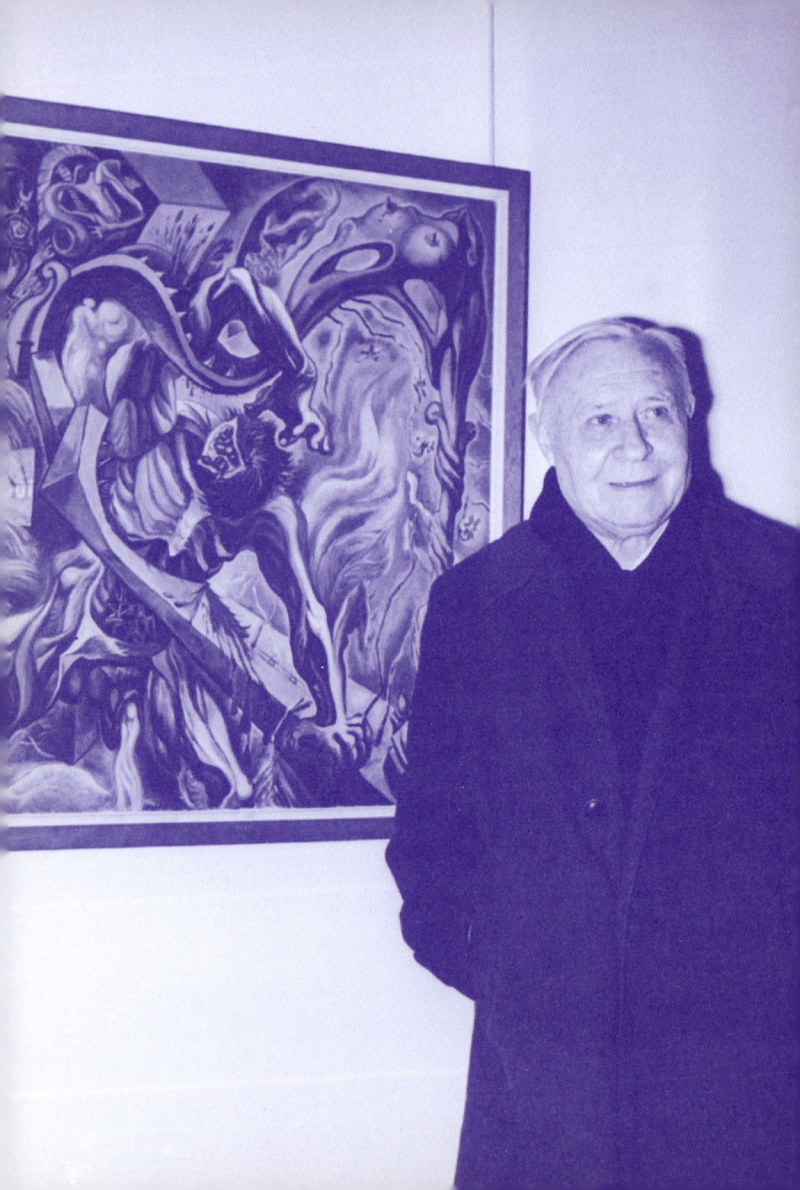

ANDRÉ MASSON

1896–1987

Place of birth/death:

Balagny-sur-Thérain, France/Paris, France

Key works:
Automatic Drawing (1924)
In the Tower of Sleep (1938)
The Metamorphosis of the Lovers (1938)
Gradiva (1939)
Pasiphaë (1942)

EARLY YEARS

André Masson was a great artist who worked across a number of different movements, although he is best remembered as one of the great Surrealist painters.

He was born in France, but his family moved to Belgium, where he was able to begin formally studying art at the Académie royale des Beaux-Arts in Brussels, when he was only 11 years old.

"Surrealism is based on eroticism."

ANDRÉ MASSON,
INTERVIEW WITH DEMOSTHENES
DAVVETAS, *ARTFORUM*,
OCTOBER 1987

ALTERED STATES

Masson entered the army during World War I, and the experience – which included his own injury – was to have a profound effect on him and his work.

After the war, he moved to Paris, France, where he was close to the Surrealist artist Joan Miró – the two even shared studio space. They became part of André Breton's Surrealist movement, and experimented with altered states of consciousness along with other like-minded artists.

"I was in the war... It horrified me, absolutely horrified me."

ANDRÉ MASSON,
INTERVIEW WITH DEMOSTHENES
DAVVETAS, *ARTFORUM*, OCTOBER 1987

STYLE AND SUBSTANCE

Masson was a keen proponent of "automatism", where the artist does not seek to consciously reproduce something on a page or canvas, instead allowing the subconscious to create. His early work was based on this principle, the most famous example being 1924's *Automatic Drawing*.

"Surrealist painters made a lot of use of psychoanalysis, of Freud. It was all mixed together."

ANDRÉ MASSON,
INTERVIEW WITH DEMOSTHENES
DAVVETAS, *ARTFORUM*,
OCTOBER 1987

COLOUR AND EMOTION

Masson's paintings are intricate and disturbing, and often angry. His work had a strong influence on Abstract Expressionists Jackson Pollock and Mark Rothko, among others, and his work occupies an important place in the evolution of modern art.

IN THE TOWER OF SLEEP

BY ANDRÉ MASSON, 1938

Location: Baltimore Museum of Art, USA

In this vivid, busy and disturbing painting, the viewer is confronted with many recurring themes of André Masson's work: eroticism, death and destruction. More than any of the Surrealists, the realism of war is visibly expressed in much of his work.

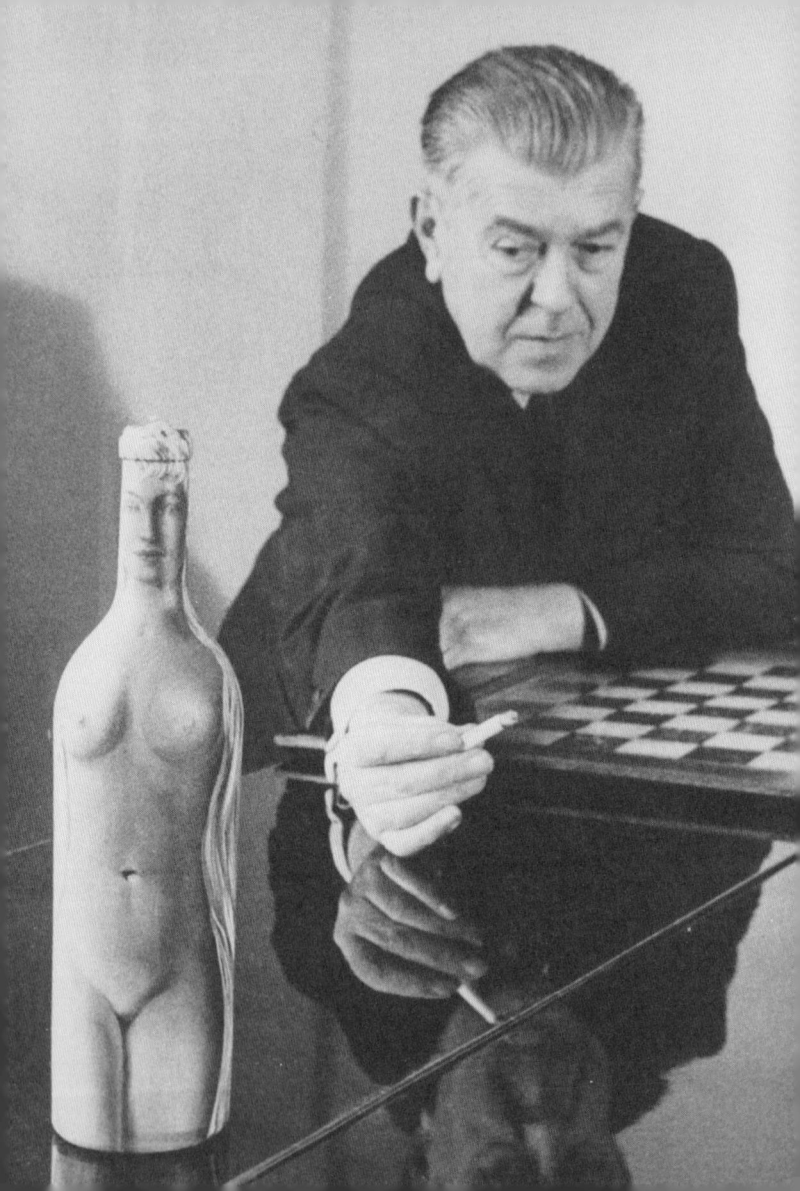

RENÉ MAGRITTE

1898–1967

Place of birth/death:

Lessines, Belgium/Brussels, Belgium

Key works:

The Menaced Assassin (1927)
The Lovers (1928)
The Treachery of Images (1929)
Golconda (1953)
The Son of Man (1964)

EARLY YEARS

Little is known of Belgian artist René Magritte's formative years, other than his mother committed suicide and that he was keen on drawing. He began formal artistic study by the time he was 18, at the Académie royale des Beaux-Arts in Brussels, and he joined the army after World War I.

In 1927, he had his first exhibition, which included his new, Surrealist paintings, but it was a disastrous event. He subsequently moved to Paris and joined André Breton's group, becoming one of the movement's leading lights.

"One of the most moving moments of my life: my eyes *saw* thought for the first time."

RENÉ MAGRITTE, ON VIEWING DE CHIRICO'S *THE SONG OF LOVE* (1914) IN 1926

INTERWAR AND BEYOND

Magritte, like Dalí, spent some time in England with the poet Edward James, who was also a Surrealist patron. Magritte then returned to Belgium, where he stayed during World War II and continued to paint. Turning to commercial art in order to make a living, his artistic career soon picked up, and he was able to work as an artist with some success for the rest of his life.

"The word 'Surrealism' doesn't mean anything to me now."

RENÉ MAGRITTE,
RENÉ MAGRITTE: SELECTED WRITINGS, 2018

THE TREACHERY OF IMAGES

BY RENÉ MAGRITTE, 1929

Location: Los Angeles County Museum of Art, USA

Also known as *This is Not a Pipe*, this work is seen as an icon of modern art. Here, René Magritte, in true enigmatic style, plays with the viewer's perceptions of, and reliance on, the experience of the image.

"Everything we see hides another thing."

RENÉ MAGRITTE,
*RENÉ MAGRITTE:
SELECTED WRITINGS*, 2018

SURREALLY POPULAR

Magritte often painted quite ordinary objects or everyday scenes but juxtaposed them in different ways, often placing them out of context. This gave his paintings a dream-like feel. It is for this reason that he is so commonly seen as the quintessential Surrealist artist, even though he did not like to be categorized in any way. In fact, many American Pop Artists of the 1960s were also influenced by Magritte, with his realistic imagery and use of everyday objects.

Today, Magritte's work is instantly recognizable and hugely popular. His *Empire of Light* (1954) sold for $121 million (£95.5 million) in 2024 – and is not even one of his most famous works.

"There are no answers in my paintings. Just questions."

RENÉ MAGRITTE,
3MINUTOSDEARTE.COM, 1965

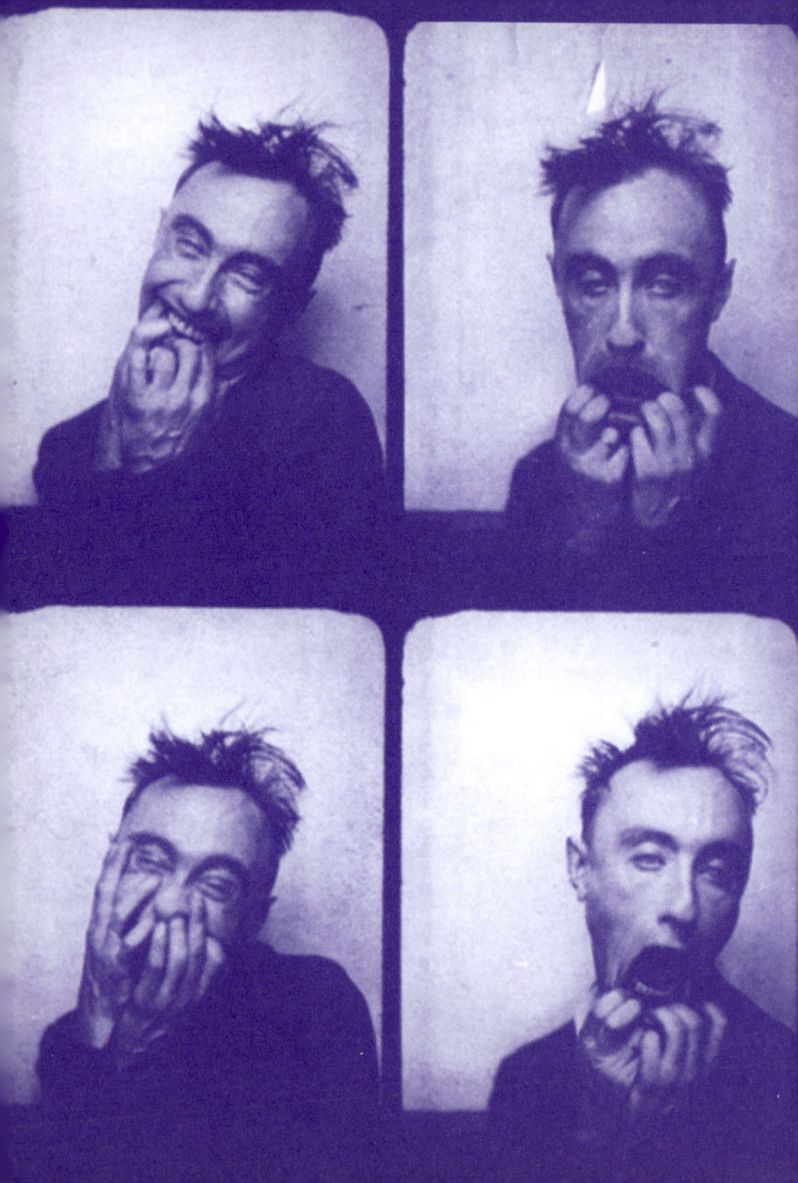

YVES TANGUY

1900–1955

Place of birth:

Paris, France/Connecticut, USA

Key works:

Mama, Papa is Wounded! (1927)
Noyer Indifférent (1929)
Indefinite Divisibility (1942)
Through Birds, Through Fire, But Not Through Glass (1943)
Rose of the Four Winds (1950)

EARLY YEARS

Yves Tanguy was not a trained artist. His father was a sailor and the family lived in Paris, spending their holidays in Finistère, on the coast of Brittany.

Tanguy's story is one of key friendships, an early one being with the poet Jacques Prévert. The two became friends in the French army around 1920. They moved to Montparnasse in Paris, where Tanguy famously saw a painting by de Chirico in a gallery window – he was utterly fascinated and decided to become a painter.

"[Tanguy's paintings] exist in a world where time, space and light are functions of other natural laws than ours."

JOHN ASHBERY,
"TANGUY – THE GEOMETER OF DREAMS",
1974

"What is Surrealism?
It is the appearance
of Yves Tanguy,
crowned with the
big emerald bird
of Paradise."

ANDRÉ BRETON, *YVES TANGUY*, 1946

SURREALISM PERSONIFIED

By 1924, Tanguy was introduced to André Breton, the author of the *Manifesto of Surrealism*. The two became very close, and the artist clearly became a favourite of the movement's leader.

Tanguy was more interested in the ideas of psychotherapist Jung than Freud, and the emphasis on dreams is clear in the artist's work, where shapes and colours are not necessarily representative of familiar objects – rather of ideas and themes.

COMMERCIAL SUCCESS

Tanguy became a popular, successful artist during the 1930s. He had exhibitions all around the world, and soon began to make a lot of money. However, being not altogether comfortable with this, by the end of the decade he had moved to the USA with his wife, Surrealist painter Kay Sage.

Alongside such artists as Max Ernst, Marc Chagall, Piet Mondrian, André Masson and Eugene Bermann, he exhibited in Pierre Matisse's Artists in Exile exhibition of 1942, featuring artists who had fled the war in Europe:

"YVES TANGUY, A SURREALIST FOR THE FUN OF IT."

JOHN RUSSELL,
THE NEW YORK TIMES,
21 JANUARY 1983

BACK IN THE USA

Tanguy remained in America – visiting Europe only once more in his life – settling and exhibiting, and he became a naturalized citizen. He continued to work until his sudden death in 1955, when he suffered a cerebral haemorrhage. His ashes were scattered in France, off the Brittany coast.

Tanguy's legacy lives on, and he was a key influence on Mark Rothko and Jackson Pollock, as well as many others.

INDEFINITE DIVISIBILITY

BY YVES TANGUY, 1942

Location: Buffalo AKG Art Museum, New York, USA

A classic piece of Surrealist art, where a dream-like scene comprises realistic but mysterious objects and shapes over a cloudy background. It flowed straight from Tanguy's imagination to create a world that defies conventional reality.

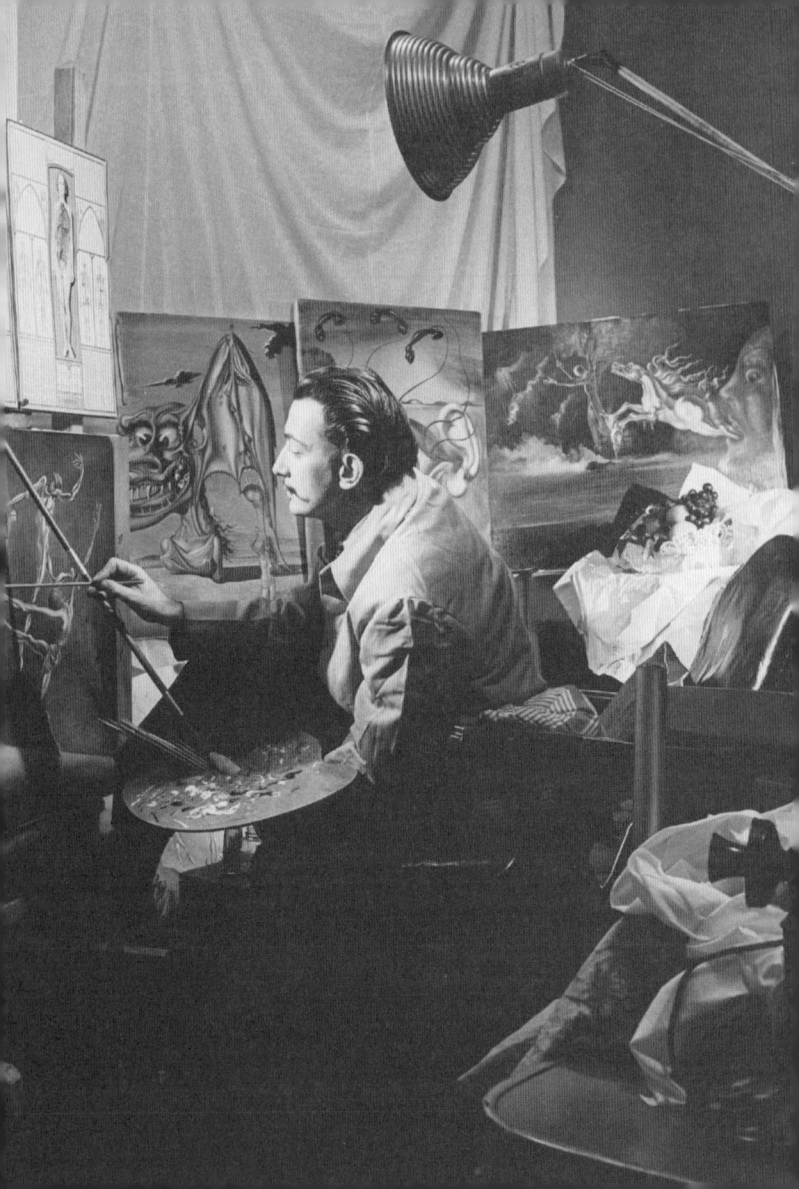

SALVADOR DALÍ

1904–1989

Place of birth/death:

Figueres, Spain/Figueres, Spain

Key works:

The Persistence of Memory (1931)
Lobster Telephone (1936)
The Elephants (1948)
Christ of Saint John of the Cross (1951)
The Sacrament of the Last Supper (1955)

EARLY YEARS

When they hear the word Surrealism, the artist most people think of is Salvador Dalí. His melting clocks, landscapes, prints and sculptures are famous the world over.

Dalí was born in Spain, north of Barcelona, and his interest and ability in art was clear from a young age. He exhibited before he was 20, and studied art in Madrid. It was there that he developed his flamboyant persona and eccentric style of dressing that are so recognizable today.

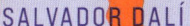
"Le Surréalisme, c'est moi" (I am Surrealism)"

SALVADORE DALÍ,
*SALVADOR DALÍ: MASTER
OF SURREALISM AND
MODERN ART* BY
G.A. CEVASCO, 1971

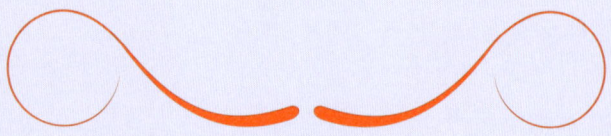

Á PARIS

Dalí's group of fellow students and friends included artists, musicians and architects, such as Luis Buñuel, Federico García Lorca, Le Corbusier and Igor Stravinsky. After Dalí was expelled from art school, he travelled to Paris. There, he joined the Surrealist movement after he had visited Pablo Picasso and studied artists such as de Chirico and Miró and the writings of Freud.

He developed his own "Paranoiac Critical Method", which involved placing himself in a paranoid state to create stunning paintings with a dream-like quality.

THE ACCOMMODATIONS OF DESIRE

BY SALVADOR DALÍ, 1929

Location: The Metropolitan Museum of Art, New York, USA

Salavador Dalí was not in the original core of Paris-based artists, yet he is probably the most famous Surrealist artist of all time. This piece is a superb demonstration of the Spanish artist's ability to portray dreams and imagination on canvas. Incorporating elements of collage into the painting, the scene is a depiction of a meander through a collection of conscious and subconscious scenarios, each expressing elements of his paranoid tendencies.

TURMOIL AND CHANGE

Throughout the 1930s, Dalí painted what would become some of his most famous works. He formed a relationship with fellow artist Paul Eluard's wife, Gala, who became his muse and, later, his wife.

Dalí was ejected from Breton's Surrealist group after a disagreement about the political developments in Spain. But he continued to create artwork, and collaborated with Englishman Sir Edward James to make, among other works, *Lobster Telephone* (1936) and the *Mae West Lips Sofa* (1937).

"It is not necessary for the public to know whether I am joking or whether I am serious, just as it is not necessary for me to know it myself."

SALVADORE DALÍ,
DIARY OF A GENIUS, 1964

EAST AND WEST

Dalí's fame grew, and he lived in the USA during and after World War II, where he branched out, making clothing, jewellery and furniture. He collaborated with Alfred Hitchcock for a famous scene in the movie *Spellbound* (1945). He returned to Europe in 1948 and continued to work there, his paintings becoming larger and more intricate in these later years.

Dalí is buried underneath his museum in Figueres, Spain, and is remembered not only as one of the greatest Surrealists, but as one of the greatest artists of all time.

"I have been inclined to regard the Surrealists as complete fools, but that young Spaniard with his candid, fanatical eyes and his undeniable technical mastery, has changed my estimate."

SIGMUND FREUD,
LETTER TO STEFAN ZWEIG, 1938

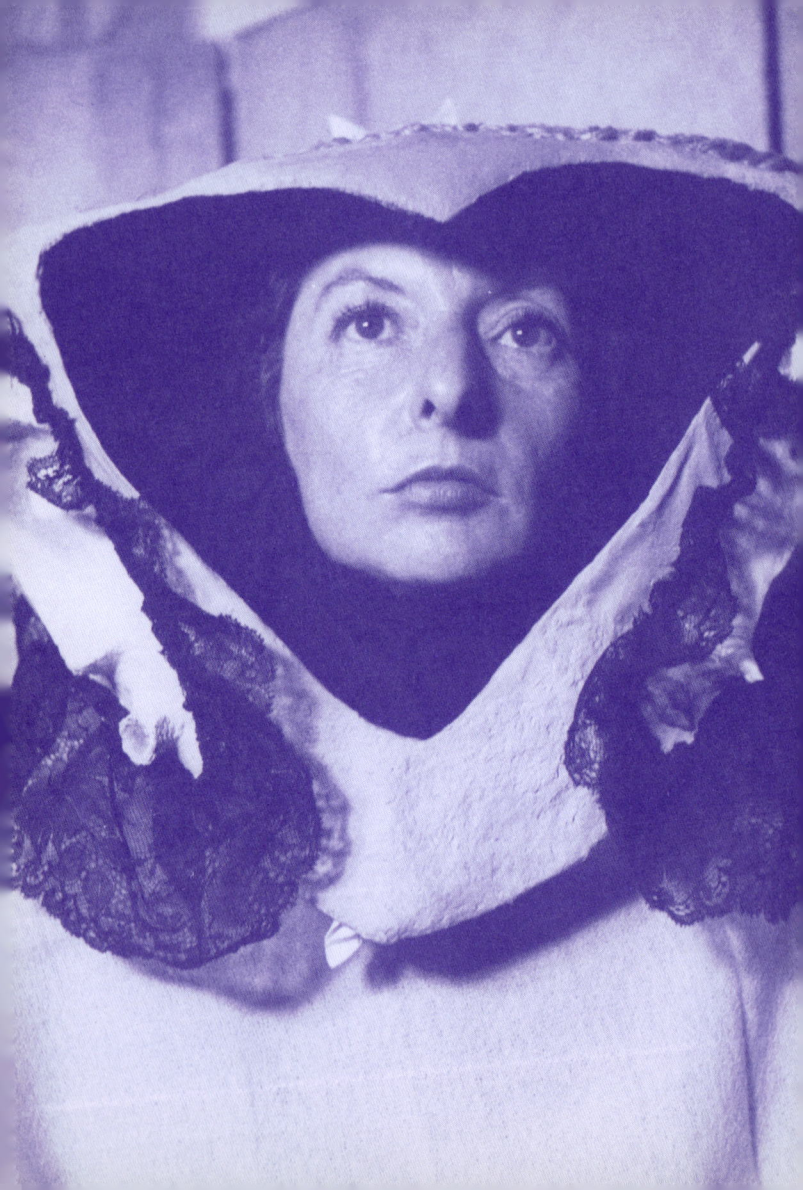

REMEDIOS VARO

1908–1963

Place of birth/death:

Girona, Spain/Mexico City, Mexico

Key works:

The Souls of the Mountain (1938)
Insomnia (1947)
Solar Music (1955)
The Juggler (1956)
Celestial Pablum (1958)

EARLY YEARS

Maria de los Remedios Alicia
Rodriga Varo y Uranga, better
known as Remedios Varo, was born
in Catalonia, northern Spain, in 1908.
From an early age, she showed an
interest in art and drawing, as well
as in mystical and spiritual themes in
art and literature. Her family moved
around Spain and north Africa when
she was young, exposing her to
different cultures and beliefs.

"One of the most important women artists associated with the Surrealist movement..."

ANNE UMLAND,
CURATOR OF PAINTING AND SCULPTURE,
INTERVIEW WITH MOMA, 2019

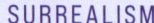

SPANISH ROOTS

In 1924, Varo attended Madrid's famous Real Academia de Bellas Artes de San Fernando, where she studied painting and drawing. She was interested in the Surrealist art scene, which involved such famous figures as Federico García Lorca, Luis Buñuel and Salvador Dalí.

"Her imagery is absolutely singular in the sense that it's inspired by magic, alchemy, transformation, and the desire to heighten self-awareness and human consciousness."

ANNE UMLAND,
CURATOR OF PAINTING AND SCULPTURE,
INTERVIEW WITH MOMA, 2019

MOVING AROUND

By 1937, Varo had lived in Paris and Barcelona, and her role as an artist was established, although not enough to earn her a living. She became a member of the Parisian Surrealist art scene and was part of the important London International Surrealist Exhibition of 1936. By 1941, Varo had fled the war in Europe and arrived in Mexico City, which became her home.

"The dream world and the real world are the same."

REMEDIOS VARO,
MOMA.ORG, 2019

STYLE AND CONTENT

Varo worked mainly with oil paint, and her dreamy subject matter is beautifully realized, often autobiographical in nature. Travel is a frequent subject, and religion and spirituality play a key part.

Varo also wrote, employing the "automatic writing" that was popular in the Surrealist movement.

ENCOUNTER

BY REMEDIOS VARO, 1959

Location: National Gallery of Scotland, Edinburgh, UK

Varo's legacy in paintings is made up of only around 100 works, many of them in private collections. This work was purchased by Scotland's National Gallery in 2023.

In this beautiful, mysterious artwork, a seated figure carefully lifts the lid on a small casket to find her own eyes staring back at her. It is a classic depiction of Varo's uncanny style, with confrontations of the self and chance meetings.

VARO AND CARRINGTON

In Mexico, Varo became a well-established artist following her first solo exhibition, which took place in 1955. She was very sought after, with a steady stream of customers for whom she supplied artwork until her untimely death in 1963.

She was very close to another of the Surrealist artists who made Mexico City their home, Leonora Carrington (for Varo portrait with mask by Carrington see *Untitled* by Kati Horna (1957) on page 92).

"Remedios seems to never limit herself to one mode of expression. For her tools of the painter and the writer are unified in breaking down our visual and intellectual customs."

KATHRYN EVERLY,
CATALAN WOMEN WRITERS AND ARTISTS: REVISIONIST VIEWS FROM A FEMINIST SPACE,
2003

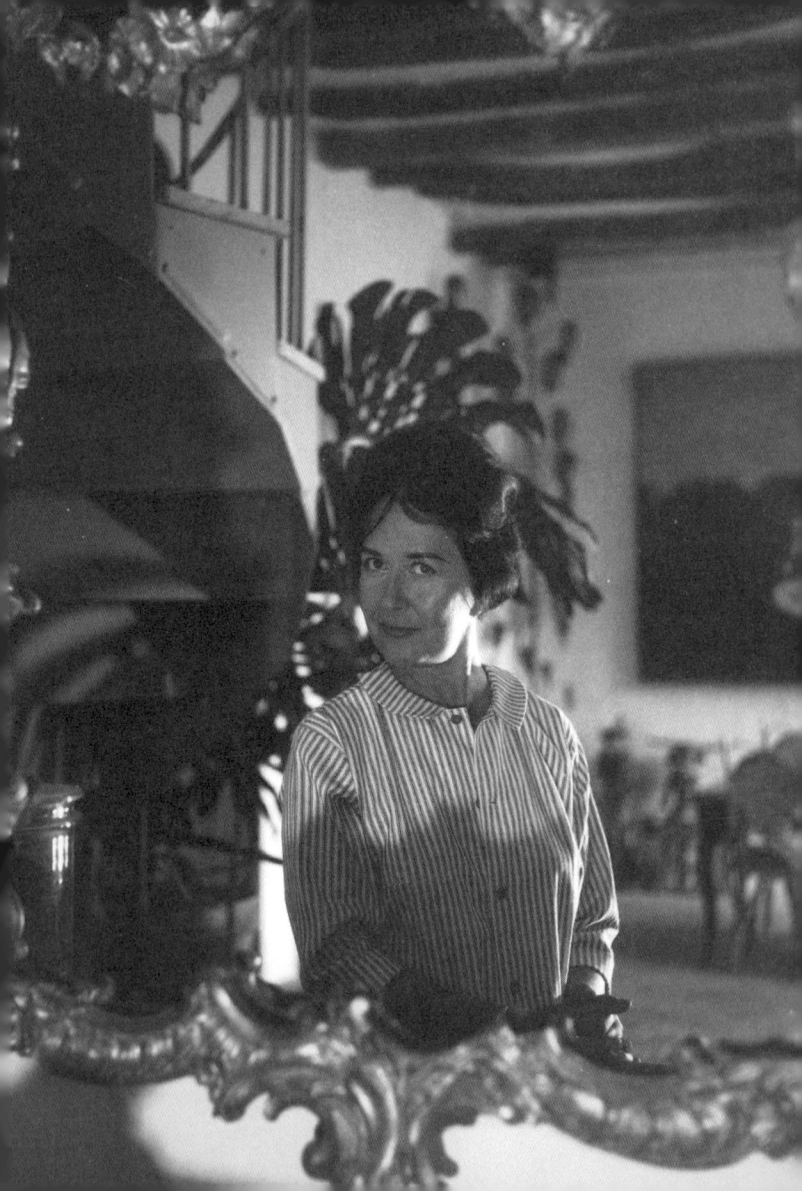

DOROTHEA TANNING

1910–2012

Place of birth/death:

Lancashire, England/Mexico City, Mexico

Key works:
Birthday (1942)
Eine Kleine Nachtmusik (1943)
Tempête en Jaune (1956)
Hôtel du Pavot, Chambre 202 (1970–73)
Etched Murmurs (1984)

EARLY YEARS

Dorothea Margaret Tanning was born in Illinois in 1910, the daughter of Swedish immigrants. Her first known foray into art came after she had worked in a library and studied at Knox College in her native Galesburg, when she left for Chicago. She moved to New York City in 1935, and began working on commercial art as well as her own personal work.

"Here is the infinitely faceted world I must have been waiting for. Here is the limitless expanse of POSSIBILITY."

DOROTHEA TANNING,
ON SEEING THE 1936 FANTASTIC ART,
DADA, SURREALISM EXHIBITION
AT MOMA, FROM *BIRTHDAY*
BY DOROTHEA TANNING, 1986

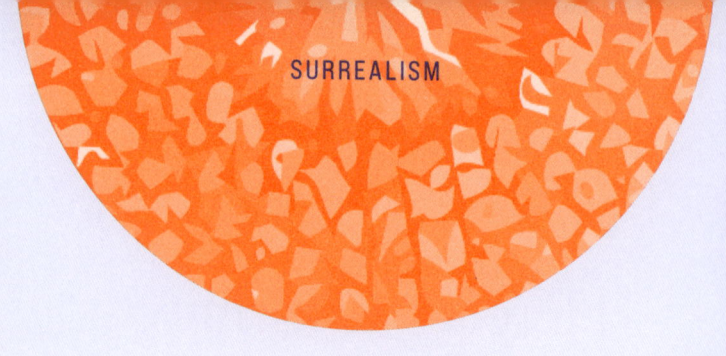

SELF-TAUGHT

Tanning only studied art for a few weeks, at the Chicago Academy of Fine Art in 1930, but she worked throughout her life as a painter, sculptor, writer and printmaker. She was extremely well-regarded and fairly successful during her lifetime, in part due to her long association with Max Ernst. But Tanning was very much an artist in her own right.

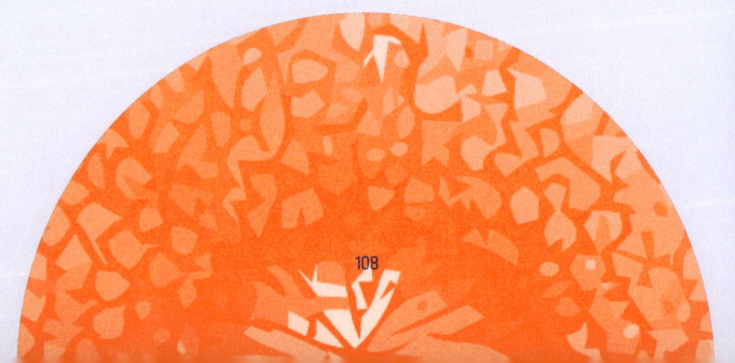

"I've always been drawn toward esoteric phenomena: the illogical, the inexpressible, the impossible."

DOROTHEA TANNING, INTERVIEW IN *BOMB* MAGAZINE, 1 OCTOBER 1990

"I have
no label
except artist."

DOROTHEA TANNING,
DOROTHEATANNING.ORG,
1989

MAX AND ME

Tanning and Max Ernst met in 1942, when he had moved to the USA because of the war in Europe. He had ended his relationship with Dorothea Carrington and was married to Peggy Guggenheim.

Ernst was fascinated by Tanning's *Birthday* (1942), and the pair married in 1946 – in a double wedding with Man Ray and Juliet Browner. They stayed together until Ernst's death in 1976.

EUROPE

Before moving to France, Tanning and Ernst lived in New York. In Sedona, Arizona, they had a house built and famously entertained many artists and writers, including Henri Cartier-Bresson, Lee Miller, Yves Tanguy, Kay Sage and Dylan Thomas.

The couple divided their time between France, New York and Sedona, until Ernst died, after which Tanning moved permanently back to the USA.

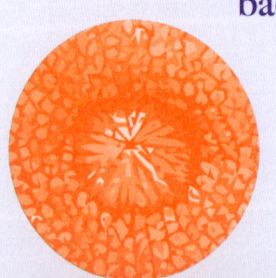
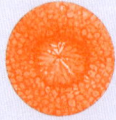

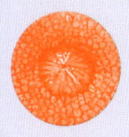

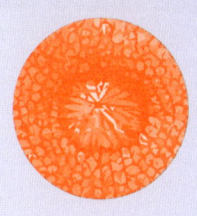

DOROTHEA TANNING

"Anything that is ordinary and frequent is uninteresting to me."

DOROTHEA TANNING,
INTERVIEW IN *BOMB* MAGAZINE,
1 OCTOBER 1990

LATER WORK

Tanning's style fitted well with the Surrealist movement, and her early works were recognizable as such, featuring intricate, detailed imagery. In later years, her work became more abstract, and she even worked in fabric (soft sculptures) for years in the 1970s.

She continued to write and paint, and her last collection of poems, *Coming to That*, was published shortly before her death at the age of 101.

BIRTHDAY

BY DOROTHEA TANNING, 1942

Location: Philadelphia Museum of Art, USA

Birthday is the work that brought Tanning to the attention of established artist Max Ernst. The surreal, yet realistic image shows the artist herself, alongside a strange creature, a winged lemur. Fantasy and reality combine, in a typically dream-like state.

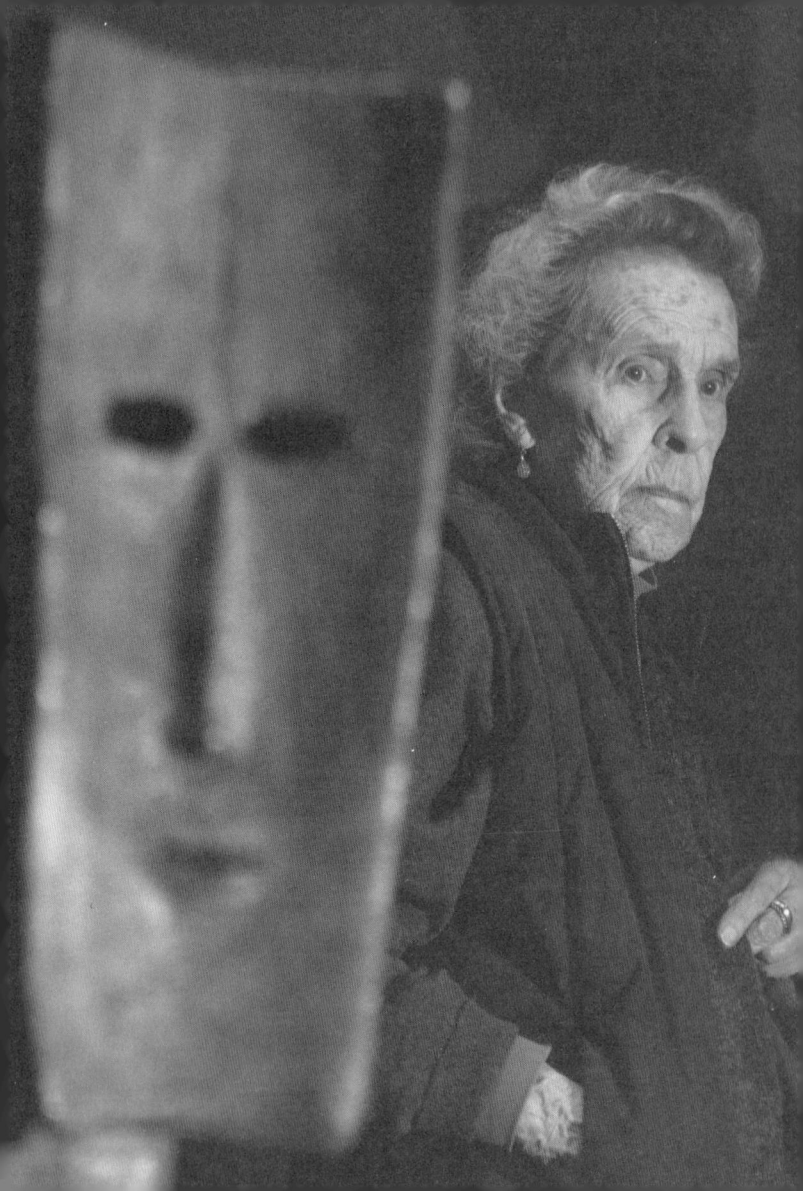

LEONORA CARRINGTON

1917–2011

Place of birth/death:

Chorley, England/Mexico City, Mexico

Key works:

Self-portrait (1937–38)
The Meal of Lord Candlestick (1938)
Portrait of Max Ernst (1939)
Ulu's Pants (1952)
Bird Bath (1974)

EARLY YEARS

Leonora Carrington was born to a wealthy family in the north of England just before the end of World War II. She was imaginative and rebellious from a very young age, and was expelled from school for her disruptive attitude and behaviour.

She travelled extensively when young, studying in Italy for a time, and saw the work of many Surrealist artists in Paris when she was just ten years old.

"Our family weren't cultured or intellectual – we were the good old bourgeoisie."

LEONORA CARRINGTON, "LEONORA AND ME" BY JOANNA MOORHEAD, THE *GUARDIAN*, 2 JANUARY 2007

"I didn't have time to be anyone's muse... I was too busy rebelling against my family and learning to be an artist."

LEONORA CARRINGTON,
FAREWELL TO THE MUSE: LOVE, WAR AND THE WOMEN OF SURREALISM
BY WHITNEY CHADWICK, 2017

DEBUTANTE

As was traditional at the time for young ladies of "society", Carrington was presented to the court of George V, where the expectation was for her to find a suitable (i.e. rich) husband. Instead, she chose to study as an artist. She was supported by the friend of many Surrealist artists, Edward James, and in 1937 she met Max Ernst.

PARIS AND BEYOND

When Max Ernst separated from his wife, he and Carrington moved to France together. They worked in paint and sculpture – famously painting portraits of each other. Leonora was also writing during this period.

When World War II broke out, Ernst moved to the safety of the USA and Carrington went to Spain; they separated and were never reunited.

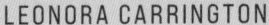

"I fell in love with Max's paintings before I fell in love with Max."

LEONORA CARRINGTON,
"LEONORA AND ME" BY JOANNA MOORHEAD,
THE *GUARDIAN*, 2 JANUARY 2007

TAKING FLIGHT

Carrington's family, fearing for her mental health, arranged for her to be taken to South Africa, after she had spent time in an asylum in Madrid. However, during a break in the journey in Portugal, she escaped her chaperone and made her way to the Mexican embassy. She married a diplomat and moved to New York, before heading to Mexico City, which she made her home until her death in 2011.

"She...
opened up a
new, and more
female, strand of
surrealism."

MATTHEW GALE,
"LEONORA AND ME" BY JOANNA
MOORHEAD, THE *GUARDIAN*,
2 JANUARY 2007

POLITICS AND PAINTING

Carrington's work, although part of the Surrealist movement, was often political and feminist in nature. Her art frequently portrayed women, but in a less traditional sense than male artists: her characters were powerful, mysterious, liberated.

Although less famous than other Surrealists, Carrington's work is beginning to be recognized, and her contribution to the world of art is immense.

THE
POCKET

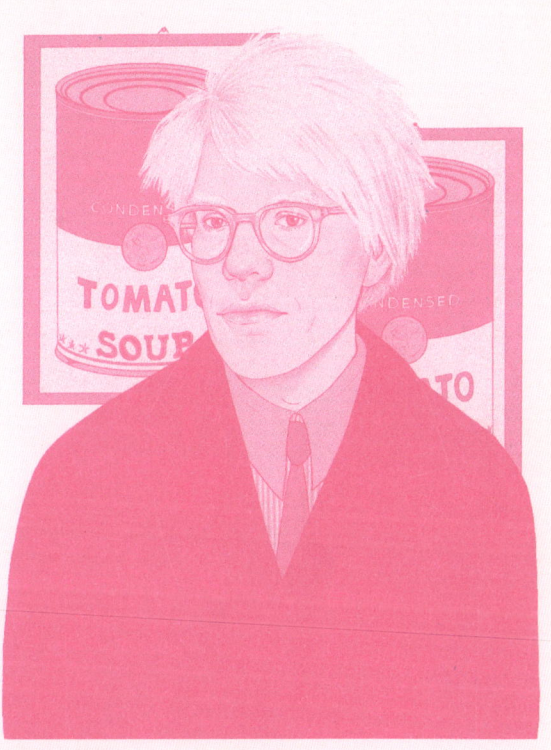

POP ART

G:

POP ART
POP ART
POP ART
POP ART
POP ART
POP ART
POP ART

CONTENTS

INTRODUCTION

Pop Art lives. In the hearts and minds of those that created it and those that admire it, and also in art, advertising and popular culture; it has never really gone away. This book provides a neat introduction to the art and artists that came to be labelled Pop Art in the 1960s – and which are still famous today.

BIRD BATH

BY LEONORA CARRINGTON, 1974

Location: Museum of Latin American Art, Long Beach, USA

Often incorporating mythical and other symbolic imagery into her work, this painting makes some reference to her experience in a mental asylum in Spain in 1940. Here, two figures dressed in black carry out a surreal baptism-like ritual with a bird in a basin of water, as they spray it with white paint.

"Surrealism was
an assault...
on the 'purity'
of painting."

ROBERT MOTHERWELL,
INTERVIEW WITH DAVID SYLVESTER, 1960

Ten artists have been selected, and although many others produced Pop Art, these were chosen because they were important, influential and long-lasting. A few of the key artworks are also highlighted, each one featuring elements of what Pop Art stood for. You may not agree with the choices, but there is no definitive list of artists and works. In fact, the who, what and where of Pop Art is argued to this day; yet another fascinating aspect of the movement...

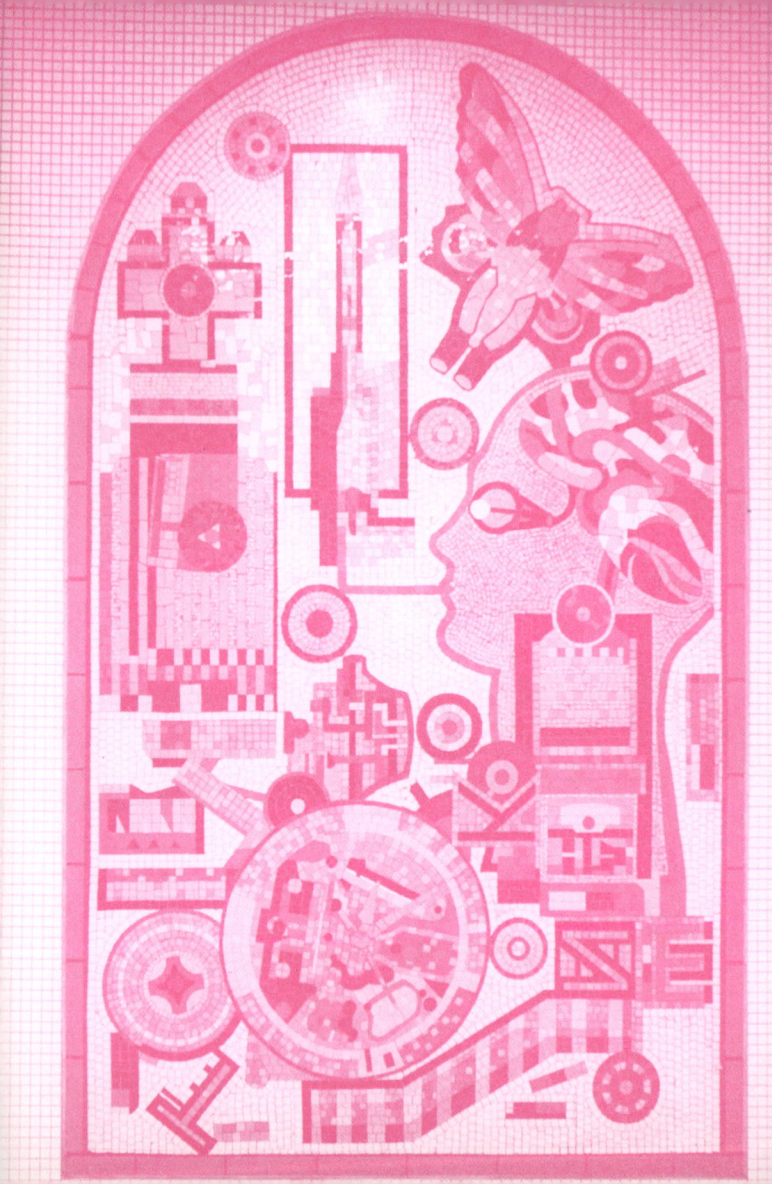

ORIGINS & INFLUENCES

WHAT IS POP ART?

Like any art movement, it depends on who you ask, and when you ask them. Founding father of the movement in Britain, Richard Hamilton, made what is probably the most widely accepted definition:

"Pop art is Popular (designed for a mass audience), Transient (short-term solution), Expendable (easily forgotten), Low Cost, Mass Produced, Young (aimed at youth), Wicked, Sexy, Gimmicky, Glamorous, Big Business."

That was in 1957. Andy Warhol – its most famous exponent – said: "it was the new Art", while the other most famous American Pop artist, Roy Lichtenstein, simply stated, "Pop Art is the use of commercial art as a subject matter in painting."

Like commercial art, Pop Art was colourful. It was young. And it had a purpose, albeit somewhat different (more aloof?) from simply making money... or did it?

REBELLIOUS ORIGINS

Pop Art had roots in many art movements, and differed depending on which side of the Atlantic Ocean you were on. British Pop Art had an ostensibly more formal origin than its American counterpart, although the two had much in common – not least the young, cultural element at its core. They shared rebellion, challenge, and a youthful mixture of celebrity, art and the everyday.

BRITISH ORIGINS

In the UK, Pop Art's birth came through the Independent Group, a collection of young artists and writers. One member, Eduardo Paolozzi (1924–2005; see his tile mosaics on page 8) – a godfather of Pop Art – created the collage *I Was a Rich Man's Plaything* in 1947. It is believed to be the first piece in which the word "pop" is actually used. The Independent Group were using the term Pop Art by 1955, and at a show in 1960 at the Royal Society of British Artists, many Pop artists were exhibiting, including Billy Apple, Peter Black and Pauline Boty.

SGT PEPPER'S LONELY HEARTS CLUB BAND

BY PETER BLAKE AND JANN HAWORTH, 1967

Possibly the most famous album cover ever produced, it was co-created by artists Peter Blake and Jann Haworth after being commissioned by the band. It features many Pop Art elements: collage, celebrity and humour. Absences from the original list of featured celebrities were Jesus and Adolf Hitler, who the record company (quite rightly) believed would cause offence.

LOVE

BY ROBERT INDIANA, 1967

Location: MoMA, New York, USA

Love was originally created in 1964 and used as the Christmas card for New York's Museum of Modern Art the following year. It is an important piece, with bold colours and strong lines that contrast with the Didone typeface, which harks back to traditional fonts of the nineteenth century.

STATESIDE

In America there was a more organic evolution. Loosely descending from Abstract Expressionism and overlapping with Neo-Dada, Pop Art marked a return (of sorts) to representational art with defined lines, bright colours and compositions. It was not until 1962 that the term hit common usage, when there was a "Symposium of Pop Art" at New York's Museum of Modern Art.

BLURRED LINES

But Pop Art – like any truly creative movement – was not static and the lines were blurred. And in the experimental heat of the post-war West, it was whatever its protagonists wanted it to be. For Ray Johnson and Peter Blake it was collage; for Jasper Johns and Robert Rauschenberg it was painting and choreography; for Andy Warhol it was screen-printing, sculpture and photography; it was any and every form of creative expression available to the artists.

There were no strict rules, and many of the artists did not even feel that they belonged to a movement – they were creating what they wanted to do, painting what they wanted to paint and expressing what they needed to express.

A BIGGER SPLASH

BY DAVID HOCKNEY, 1967

Location: Private ownership

An important painting in the evolution
of both British art and Pop Art, this
piece is more allied to traditional
artforms than the Pop Art collages
and screen prints that preceded it.
But the strong lines and bold colours
demonstrate its links to the movement,
and Hockney (1937–) is one of its most
important, later era artists.

ART & CULTURE INFLUENCES

Pop Art had multiple influences, including commercial art, advertising, celebrity culture and consumerism. There were many different artists and many different mediums. And Pop Art is still being created, but instead of the daring, counter-culture pieces that commented on what was happening to modern society, it has become part of the establishment it once critiqued; frequently seen in advertising; another sales technique.

But what is any art if it's not something to be looked at and reflected upon? It is a commodity, and always has been. Maybe Pop Art was simply honest.

CATEGORIZATION

And regarding the label: "No one of them liked that term [Pop Art] ", said James Rosenquist's widow, Mimi. "They all said, 'What does that mean?' because they were all so different."

Therein lies the issue: although Pop Art is viewed as one single movement, with a definition, a beginning and (almost) an end, it is not actually that simply formulated and easy to categorize. Not everything is what it seems to be, and what you see is not always what you get.

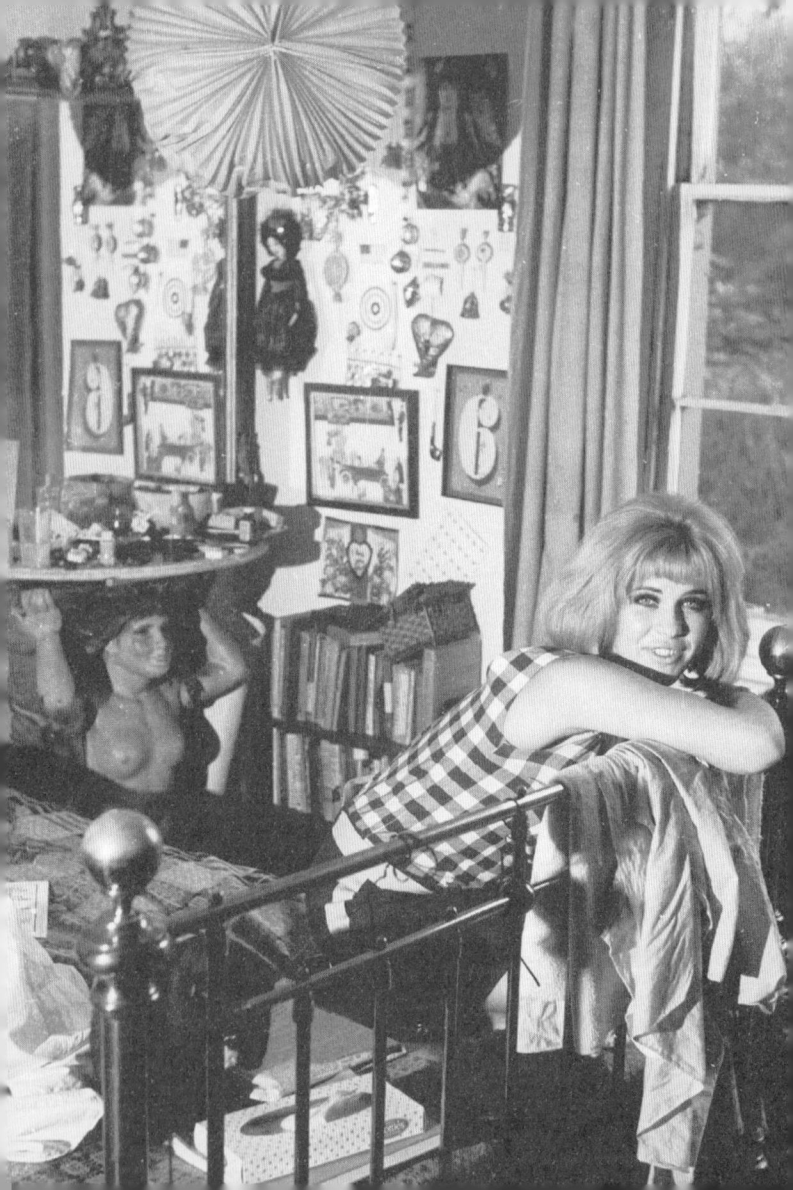

PAULINE BOTY

1938–1966

Place of birth/death:

Carshalton, England/London, England

Key works:

The Only Blonde in the World (1963)
Untitled (red yellow blue abstract) (c. 1961)
It's a Man's World I (1964)
*What we need now to discover in the social realm
is the moral equivalent of war...* (1964)
Siren (c. 1958–1962)

EARLY YEARS

Boty was born in Surrey in England in 1938, the youngest of four in a typical middle-class family. Her mother supported her artistic endeavours (her father didn't), but Pauline earned a scholarship to study art at Wimbledon School of Art in South London, and was able to attend.

She studied lithography and stained glass as well as painting and collage. The famous exhibition Young Contemporaries in 1957 featured one of her pieces. As well as creating art, Boty also danced, sang and wrote poetry.

SWINGING SIXTIES

Boty featured in *Pop Goes the Easel*,
a documentary about the Young
British Artists of the era, directed
by Ken Russell. And she was part of
a wider group of young, left-leaning
figures from art and the media. She
married Clive Goodwin in 1963
(after, famously, meeting him ten
days' earlier) and their apartment
in London was frequented by
many prominent figures of the
time, including Peter Blake, David
Hockney, Dennis Potter, Roger
McGough – and even Bob Dylan.

"All over the country young girls are starting, shouting and shaking, and if they terrify you, they mean to and they are beginning to impress the world."

PAULINE BOTY,
THE PUBLIC EAR, BBC, 1967

KEY FIGURE

Pauline Boty became a central figure in British Pop Art, and her work involved politics, female roles in society and popular culture. She featured celebrities such as Marilyn Monroe, John-Paul Belmondo and Elvis Presley in her work. Boty used painting, collage, drawing, lithograph and stained glass, and she fought the sexism that was inherent in society at that time, giving a female-positive viewpoint to her art. Many of her paintings were often sensual, and celebratory of female sexuality.

Her importance was little known until the last decade of the 20th century. Now her significant contribution to both art and feminism is being recognized.

Boty's 1964 work
(to give it its full title)

**WHAT WE NEED NOW TO
DISCOVER IN THE SOCIAL REALM
IS THE MORAL EQUIVALENT
OF WAR; SOMETHING HEROIC
THAT WILL SPEAK TO MAN
AS UNIVERSALLY AS WAR
DOES, AND YET WILL BE AS
COMPATIBLE WITH THEIR
SPIRITUAL SELVES AS WAR HAS
PROVED TO BE INCOMPATIBLE**

referred to a quote by William James.
It is owned by the Smithsonian
American Art Museum in
Washington, DC, USA,
although it is not on view.

"Boty enriched Pop Art by bringing together celebration and critique in a way no one had done before."

PAULINEBOTY.ORG

MULTI-TASKER

More than an exhibiting artist, she was also an actress. Boty appeared on various stage and big and small screens in the 1960s including the classic movie *Alfie* (1966) with Michael Caine. She was a dancer on the pop music show *Ready Steady Go!*

Boty died in 1966 aged only 28, shortly after giving birth to her daughter. She was diagnosed with cancer after early prenatal tests, but she refused treatment until her daughter was born.

Boty created around 100 pieces, only 40 of which are thought to have survived, including art of various mediums.

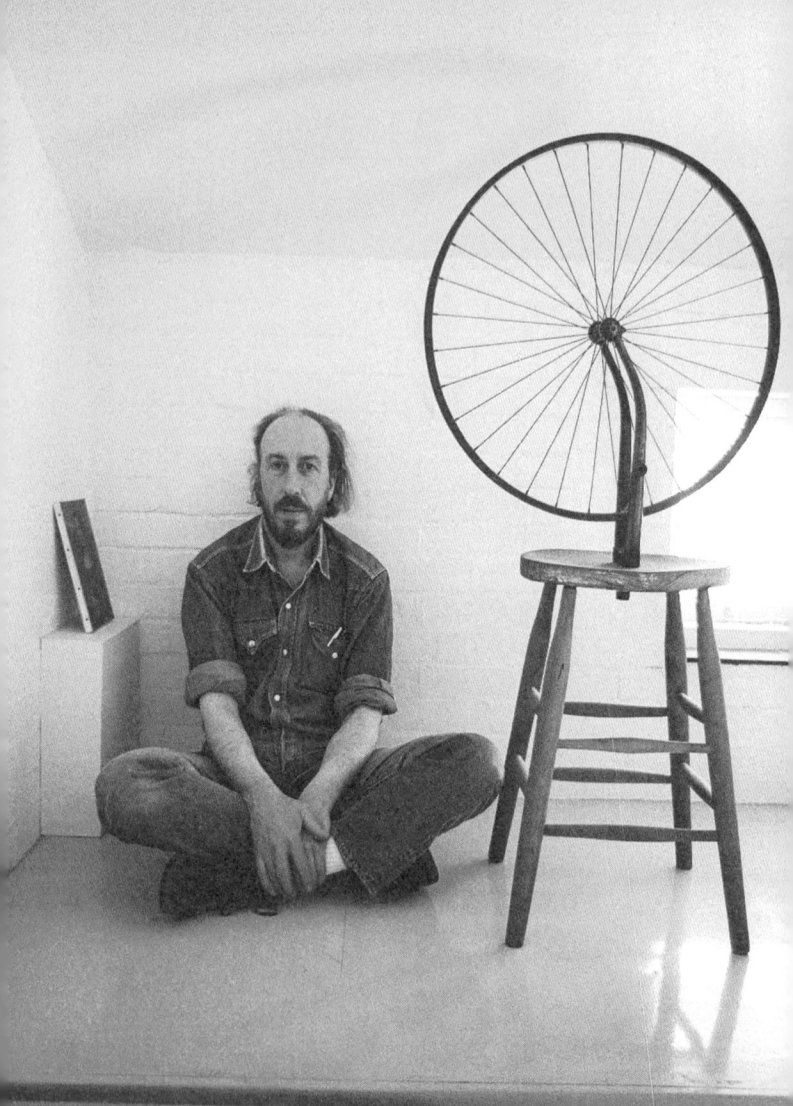

RICHARD HAMILTON

1922–2011

Place of birth/death:

London, England/London, England

Key works:

*Just what is it that makes today's homes
so different, so appealing?* (1956)
*Towards a definitive statement on the coming
trends in men's wear and accessories
(a) Together let us explore the stars* (1962)
Swingeing London 67 (1967–68)
Shock and Awe (2007–08)

EARLY YEARS

Richard Hamilton was born in
Pimlico, London, in 1922. When he
left school he had no qualifications
and worked for a firm that supplied
electrical components. But he had
obvious artistic talent, and later
attended Saint Martin's School of
Art, the Westminster School of Art
and the Royal Academy of Arts –
all in London.

SERIOUS STUDY

Following a break for the war, in which he made technical drawings for the military, Hamilton returned to the Royal Academy, which was run at the time by Sir Alfred Munnings (1878–1959), who was famously critical of modern art. It was not long before Hamilton was expelled and therefore had to complete two years' national service, which he undertook in the Royal Engineers.

He later attended Slade School of Art in London, and in 1951 he exhibited some pieces in an exhibition at the Institute of Contemporary Arts entitled Growth and Form, which was opened by the Swiss-French architect Le Corbusier (1887–1965).

"The artist in twentieth-century urban life is inevitably a consumer of mass culture and potentially a contributor to it."

RICHARD HAMILTON,
RICHARD HAMILTON: COLLECTED WORKS, 1982

JUST WHAT IS IT THAT MAKES TODAY'S HOMES SO DIFFERENT, SO APPEALING?

BY RICHARD HAMILTON, 1956

Location: Kunsthalle Tübingen, Germany

One of the most famous images of British post-war art, and a poster for the Pop Art genre, the collage was originally created by the artist for an exhibition catalogue. Many of the sources are American magazines and advertisements, including *Ladies' Home Journal* and *Tomorrow's Man*. This repurposing of material, demonstrating the disposable culture of contemporary society, was a key element in Pop Art.

CELEBRITY CONTACTS

During travel to the USA, Hamilton became close to the artist Marcel Duchamp (1887–1968), and in 1966 organized a major retrospective of the artist's work in London.

Hamilton taught Brian Ferry, the founder of Roxy Music, and became friendly with Paul McCartney of the Beatles. Hamilton designed the cover of *The Beatles* (the "White Album"). Latterly, Hamilton embraced new technologies and continued to push the boundaries of art, politics and expression.

"All art is equal – there was no hierarchy of value. Elvis was to one side of a long line while Picasso was strung out on the other side..."

RICHARD HAMILTON,
RICHARD HAMILTON: COLLECTED WORKS, 1982

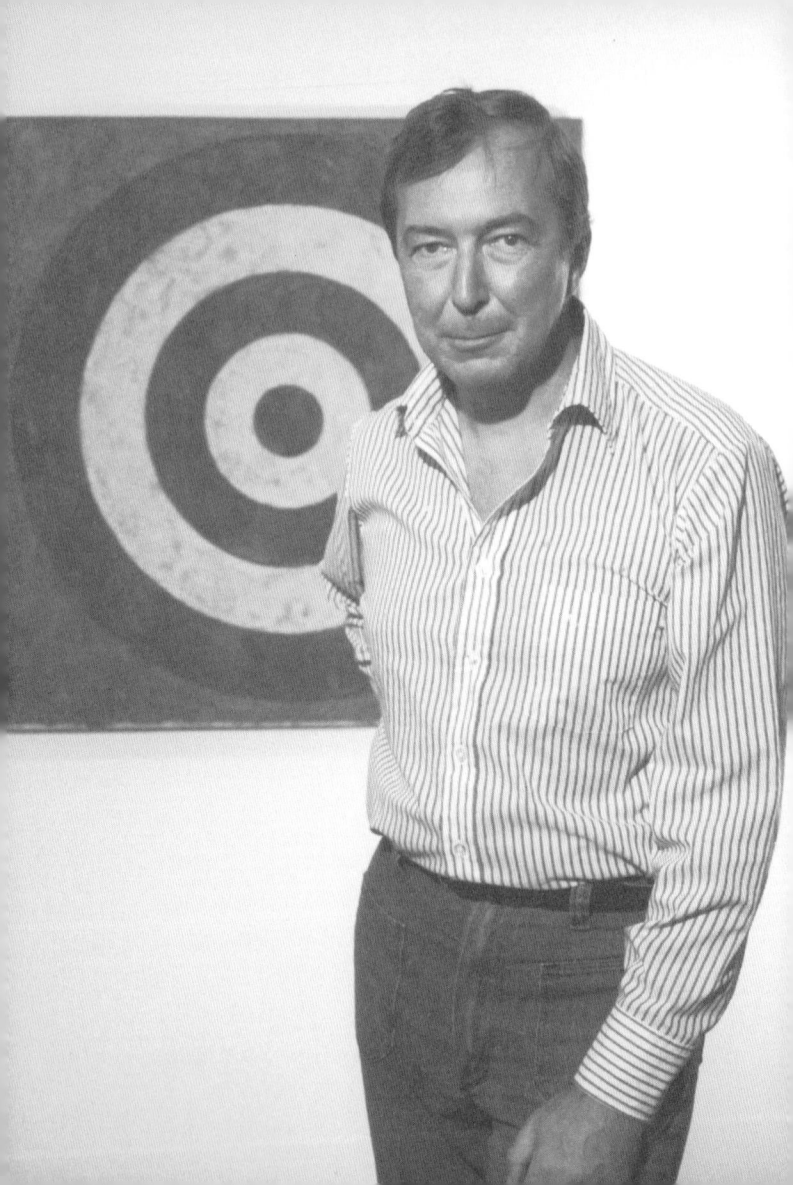

JASPER JOHNS

1930–

Place of birth:

Augusta, Georgia, USA

Key works:

Flag (1954–55)
Target with Four Faces (1955)
False Start (1959)
Painted Bronze (Ale Cans) (1960)
Corpse and Mirror II (1974)

EARLY YEARS

Jasper Johns was born in Augusta, Georgia, in 1930, but he spent his early years in South Carolina with his grandparents after his parents' divorce. He studied at the University of South Georgia from 1947–48 but moved to New York City soon afterwards at the suggestion of his teacher.

He started at Parsons School of Design but left soon after and was drafted into the army, serving in the USA and Japan.

By 1953 Johns was back in New York City, where he met fellow artist Robert Rauschenberg. The two enjoyed a romantic and artistic relationship, and shared studio space.

"It is in this period [1954] that I matured a bit and became a functioning artist."

JASPER JOHNS,
THE ART NEWSPAPER, 2007

FLAG

BY JASPER JOHNS, 1954–55

Location: MoMA, New York, USA

An early example, Johns' piece was one of more than 40 works he created that were based on the national flag of the United States, which also included *White Flag* in 1955 and *Three Flags* in 1958. At the time, this work was seen as a political piece, possibly critical of the USA, but contemporary and subsequent popularity demonstrates this is not the case; it is more about the flag as an article, motif and symbol.

DESTRUCTION & DREAMS

In 1954, Johns destroyed all of his existing artwork in order to start anew and leave Abstract Expressionism behind him. Shortly afterwards, he was inspired by a dream in which he saw the American flag and the next day he created an artwork of it. Johns painted and created many other artworks based on the stars and stripes.

In 1958 Johns mounted his first solo exhibition, in New York. *Flag* was featured, alongside various other works. It was a big success, and the Museum of Modern Art acquired some of the art – a rare occurrence for such a young, unknown artist.

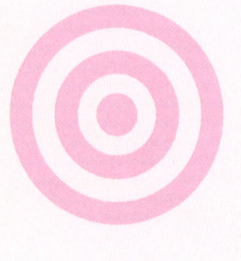

POPULAR & POP

Many of Johns' early works featured
bright colours and images, which
allied him to the Pop Art movement
in America, but he moved on
from such work, becoming more
introspective in his later years, when
he created many prints
and sculptures too.

COLLECTABLE

Johns is one of the world's bestselling artists, despite keeping himself out of the limelight. *Flag* sold for $110 million in 2010 and Johns received the Presidential Medal of Freedom in 2011.

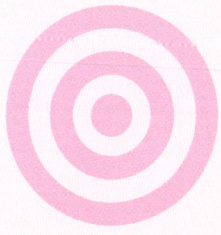

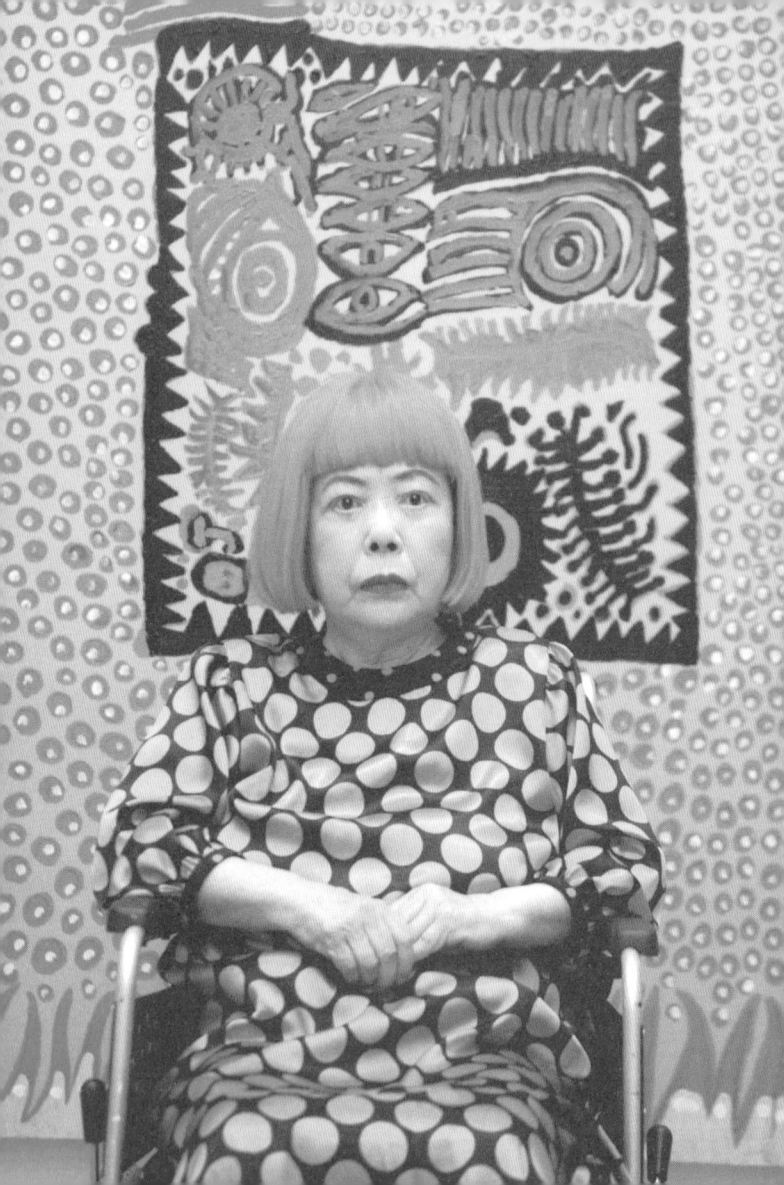

YAYOI KUSAMA

1929–

Place of birth:

Matsumo, Japan

Key works:

Infinity Mirror Room – Phalli's Field (1965)
Narcissus Garden (1966)
Pumpkin (1990s onwards)
Fireflies on the Water (2002)
My Eternal Soul (2009 onwards)

EARLY YEARS

Yayoi Kusama was born in Japan in 1929 – between two world wars – and the events of her early life were to inspire her to art, fame and fortune. She was raised in Matsumoto and from a very young age was painting and drawing, including images of pumpkins for which she is still famous today. Her parents did not encourage her, and Japanese society was not welcoming to art that was anything other than traditional.

"My art originates from hallucinations only I can see. I translate the hallucinations and obsessional images that plague me into sculptures and paintings."

YAYOI KUSAMA,
BOMB, WINTER 1999

"The sexual obsession and fear of sex sit side by side in me."

YAYOI KUSAMA,
FINANCIAL TIMES, 2012

ART FROM MISERY

There are a few key elements and events that made Kusama the artist she is today. According to her autobiography, her father had many extramarital affairs and she witnessed sexual encounters between him and other women. This led to a life-long fear of sex, which became a key theme in her subsequent art journey.

Around the age of ten, Kusama began to suffer vivid hallucinations, which manifested themselves as series of dots. In order to deal with the reality of them, and to escape, Kusama drew dot images.

She studied painting in Kyoto just after World War II, but she was more interested in contemporary art from the USA and Europe. Her style of signature dot patterns began to emerge in the 1950s. She referred to these patterns as "infinity nets" and she has said they were taken directly from what she experienced in her hallucinations.

"I fight pain, anxiety and fear every day, and the only method I have found that relieves my illness is to keep creating art."

YAYOI KUSAMA, *INFINITY NET: THE AUTOBIOGRAPHY OF YAYOI KUSAMA*, 2003

NEW YORK

After living in Tokyo and Europe, Kusama moved to the USA, around 1957. She was first based in Seattle, but moved to New York City a year later, where she became part of the evolving modern art and performance scene. A very political artist, her work in the States included "happenings" that protested against, frequently, the Vietnam War. Her work was very provocative and challenged perceptions of art and its function.

Kusama exhibited various pieces in multiple forms, including photography, sculpture and painting. She created a series of *Infinity Mirror Rooms* where lights and mirrors combined with music to make immersive, interactive sculptures that engaged multiple senses in the viewer.

"Kusama's *Infinity Mirror Rooms*' decidedly analogue processes of reflection underscore the idea that communication itself remains visual art's most vital endeavour."

GLORIA SUTTON,
THE ARCHITECTURAL REVIEW, 2021

SELF-TREATMENT

Kusama returned to Japan in 1973, and struggled with mental health issues. By 1977 she found treatment, part of which included living in a hospital, something she does to this day. Subsequently, she has become a hugely successful artist. Her large sculptures and interactive pieces have ensured her stature in the art world and retrospectives of her work are common.

"Even after
I finish my life,
I'd like to keep
telling posterity
about my way
of art."

YAYOI KUSAMA,
TATE MODERN, 2021

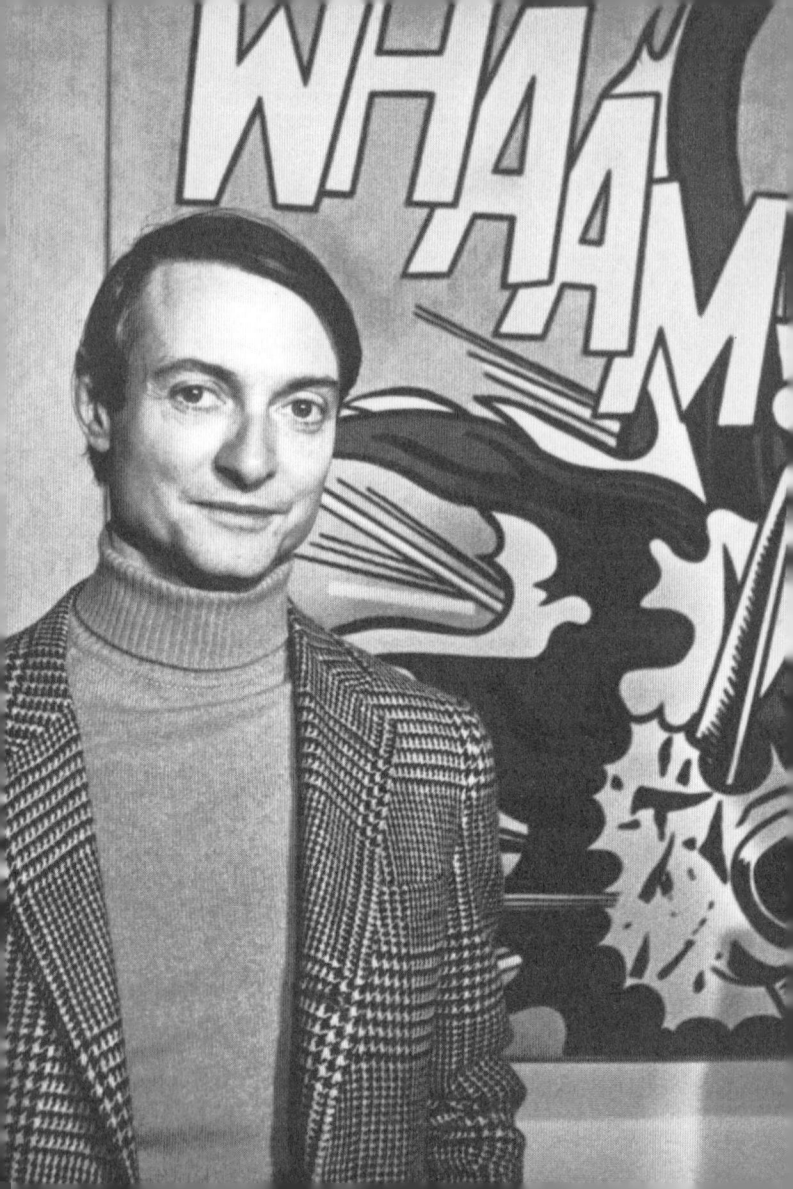

ROY LICHTENSTEIN

1923–1997

Place of birth/death:

New York, NY, USA/New York, NY, USA

Key works:

Look Mickey (1961)
Masterpiece (1962)
Whaam! (1963)
Drowning Girl (1963)
Oh, Jeff... I Love You, Too... But... (1964)

EARLY YEARS

Roy Lichtenstein was born in New York City in 1923. His parents were of German heritage and the family was comfortably off, living in the city's Upper West Side. The young Roy was a jazz fan, keen on drawing from a young age.

Lichtenstein started a course at Ohio State University after he left school, but stopped as he worked in the army for three years, from 1943 until after the end of World War II. Thanks to the GI Bill, which allowed ex-servicemen to study (among other things), he was able to return to Ohio and he graduated with a Master's in Fine Art in 1949.

RAPID RISER

Lichtenstein's rise to fame was rapid; by 1962 his first solo show, at New York's Castelli Gallery, was a huge success – everything was sold before the doors even opened. It was not long before he stopped teaching and concentrated on his artistic career full-time.

Lichtenstein was the first American artist to be exhibited at the Tate Gallery in London, in 1964.

A TRUE POP ARTIST

By 1960, Lichtenstein was lecturing at Rutgers University in New Jersey, and he started painting his first "pop" artworks. Apparently one of Lichtenstein's sons asked his dad if he could paint as well as the images in a cartoon, and this provided the inspiration for his first use of imagery with oversize dots: *Look Mickey* (1961).

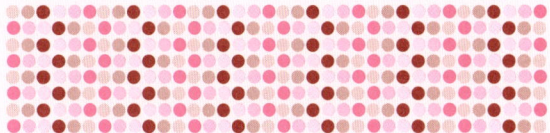

BEN-DAY
DOTS

The printing process to create many colours from four inks was developed in 1879 by Benjamin Day Jr. Known as Ben-Day Dots, different coloured dots are spaced around an image to create the illusion of many different colours and shades. Commonly seen in comic books, Lichtenstein used the system in his early artworks.

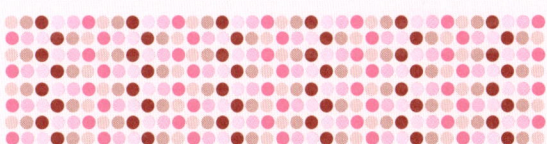

"Pop art looks out into the world. It doesn't look like a painting of something, it looks like the thing itself."

ROY LICHTENSTEIN,
INTERVIEW WITH GENE SWENSON, 1963

WHAAM!

BY ROY LICHTENSTEIN, 1963

Location: Tate Modern, London, England

One of the paintings that could be used as a wordless answer if someone asked what Pop Art is, *Whaam!* demonstrates Lichtenstein's method of blowing up a small cartoon into something bigger, encouraging focus on what it has become. The original panel was drawn by Irv Novick (1916–2004) for the magazine *All-American Men of War* in 1962. A diptych, *Whaam!* is part of a series of war paintings Lichtenstein worked on from 1962 to 1964.

GLOBAL SUCCESS

It was during the early 1960s that the paintings that Lichtenstein is most famous for were created. His style involved the reproduction of a comic book frame image and enlarging it massively. This led to discussion in artistic circles about what art was, what it stood for, and how Lichtenstein's work fitted in. Given his enduring popularity (not to mention the huge prices paid for his work), it seems incredible today that his artistic integrity was challenged.

"I think my work
is different from
comic strips – but
I wouldn't call it
transformation;
I don't think that
whatever is meant
by it is important
to art."

ROY LICHTENSTEIN,
INTERVIEW WITH GENE SWENSON, 1963

"I am nominally copying, but I am really restating the copied thing in other terms."

ROY LICHTENSTEIN, TATE MODERN

ORIGINALITY

Rather than being critiqued in terms of style, originality and commentary on mass-produced popular culture, much of the discussion of Lichtenstein's work was about how much he was relying on the original works that he based many of his artworks on. Comic book artists at that time were largely anonymous; very few were credited, and the medium was far removed from the acceptance it enjoys today.

Subsequently, Lichtenstein has been acknowledged as a pioneer of a medium as well as a trailblazer in terms of comment on society and popular culture. In later years, his work referred to the art of such European painters as Pablo Picasso, Henri Matisse and Salvador Dalí.

MULTIMEDIA

Although most famous as a painter, Lichtenstein worked with sculpture and even made a movie. In 1969 he created artwork for a suite at the Palace Hotel in St Moritz, Switzerland; in 1977 he decorated a BMW (known as the *Art Car*); and in 1994 he created a mural in the Times Square subway in New York. He even created the *DreamWorks Logo* (1996) for DreamWorks Records, which turned out to be his final project.

Lichtenstein's foundation lists more than 5,000 artworks created by him, including paintings, woodwork, sculpture, collage and prints, as well as photographs of the artist at work from all eras of his extensive career.

Lichtenstein's *Masterpiece* (1962) sold for $165 million in 2017 and was the most expensive sale of the artist's work.

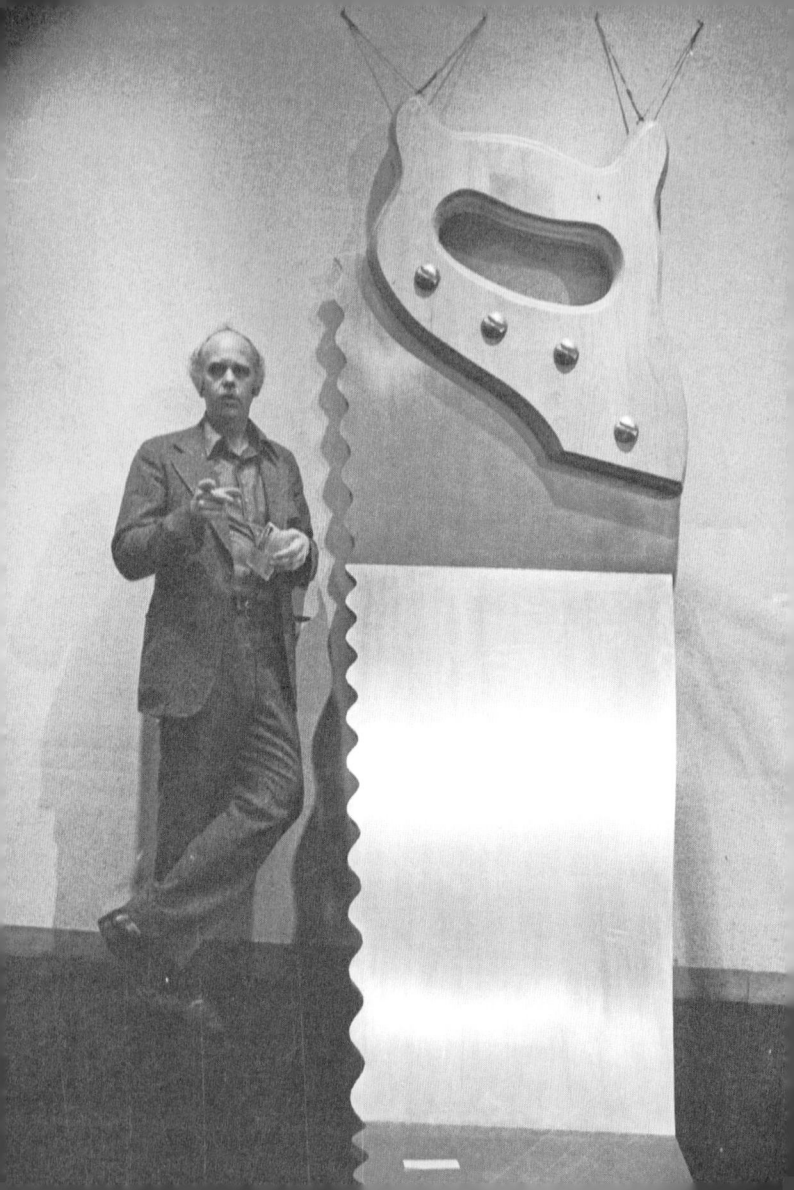

CLAES OLDENBURG

1929–2022

Place of birth/death:

Stockholm, Sweden/New York, NY, USA

Key works:

Pastry Case I (1961–62)
Floor Cake, (1962)
Soft Toilet (1966)
Lipstick (Ascending) on Caterpillar Tracks (1969)
Clothespin (1976)
Spoonbridge and Cherry (1988)

EARLY YEARS

Born in Sweden in 1929, Oldenburg lived in the USA from 1936 because his father was a diplomat. He grew up in Chicago and attended Yale University. He became a naturalized US citizen in 1953 and moved to New York.

He performed at "happenings" – partly improvised artistic performances – in the 1960s, calling his group Ray Gun Theatre. He worked with various other artists too, including Jim Dine, Allan Kaprow and Tom Wesselmann.

"My rule was not to paint things as they were. I wasn't copying; I was remaking them as my own."

CLAES OLDENBURG,
INTERVIEW MAGAZINE, 2015

SOFT SCULPTURES

Oldenburg started to produce his famous soft sculptures in the late 1950s, making letters, figures and food. He worked with his first wife Patty Mucha (1935–), who sewed many of his works; Warhol painted her in the work *Patty Oldenburg* (1962).

In 1961 Oldenburg rented a shopfront in Manhattan and filled it with soft sculptures of food and consumer products. This was named *The Store*, and was a very important event in not only his career, but also in the evolution of art – Pop Art.

FOOD FOR THOUGHT

At this time in his career Oldenburg was most famous for creating large, everyday objects from various soft materials, including foodstuffs and packaging. MoMA acquired his plaster and paint piece from 1962, *Two Cheeseburgers, with Everything (Dual Hamburgers)*. He worked closely with his second wife, Coosje van Bruggen (1942–2009), a Dutch-American sculptor and critic.

BIGGER PICTURE

From the 1970s onwards, Oldenburg concentrated on producing oversized outdoor sculptures, often of large-scale objects seemingly at odds with their surroundings. Examples include a huge garden trowel for *Trowel I* (1971) in Otterlo, the Netherlands; skittles and a bowling ball for *Flying Pins* (2000) in Eindhoven, the Netherlands; and a giant ice cream cone for *Dropped Cone* (2001), in Cologne, Germany.

"I am for art that is put on and taken off like pants, which develops holes like socks, which is eaten like a piece of pie, or abandoned with great contempt like a piece of shit."

CLAES OLDENBURG, *I AM FOR...*, 1961

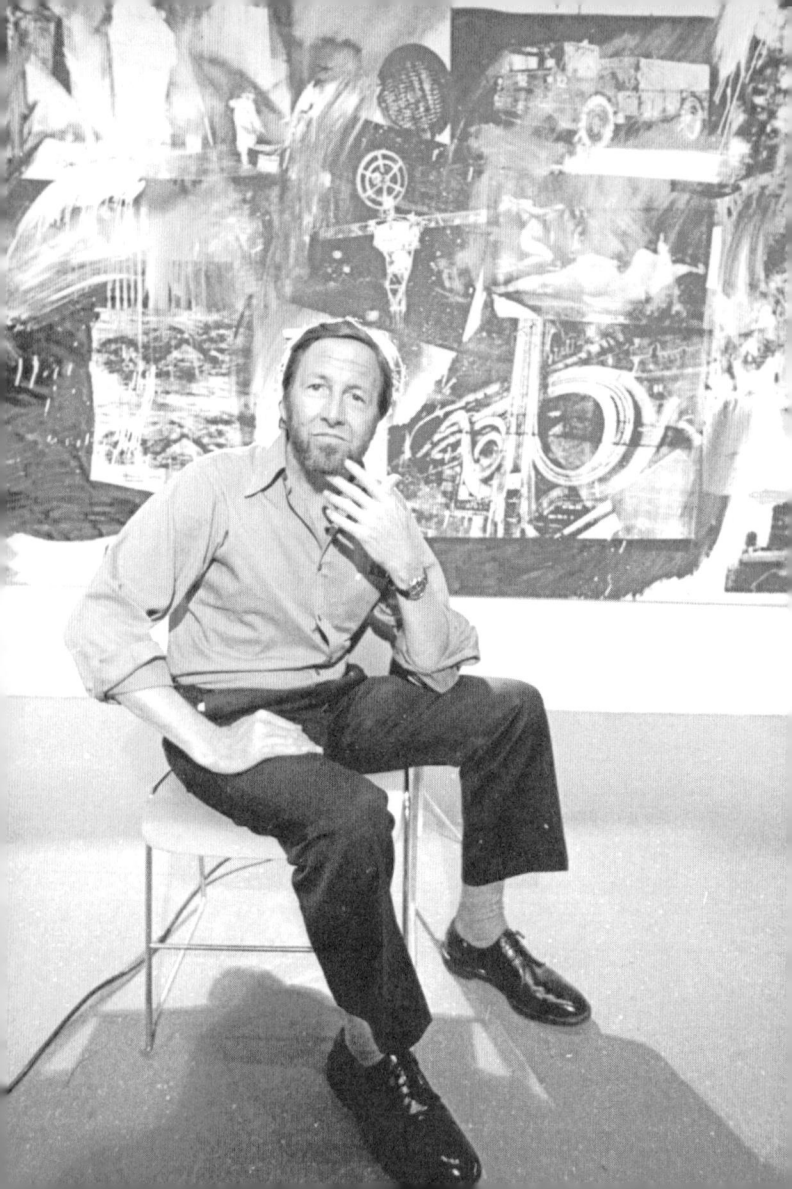

ROBERT RAUSCHENBERG

1925–2008

Place of birth/death:

Port Arthur, Texas, USA/Florida, USA

Key works:

White Paintings (1951)
Bed (1955)
Skyway (1964)
Signs (1970)

EARLY YEARS

Milton Ernest Rauschenberg was born in Texas in 1925. His paintings and graphic art contributed massively to the Pop Art movement in the USA in the 1960s, and he continued to work in various mediums until his death in 2008.

The Rauschenberg family was poor. Milton's father had a job at Gulf State Utilities, but times were hard. As a boy, Milton was interested in drawing, particularly cartoons, but he did no art seriously in his youth.

WAR & PEACE

Milton enrolled at the University of Texas in Austin to study pharmacology in 1943, as war was raging around the world. He was drafted and became a medical technician in a Navy hospital, stationed in California.

After the war ended and he was discharged from the army, Rauschenberg changed his name to Robert, although he was commonly referred to as Bob. He started at the Kansas City Art Institute and also studied in Paris at the Académie Julian.

ART
CLASS

In 1948 Rauschenberg
enrolled at Black Mountain
College in North Carolina
and studied under the tutelage
of the famously strict artist
Josef Albers. While there, he
met music and dance artists
who were to become lifelong
friends, John Cage and Merce
Cunningham. Together with
Jasper Johns, they were labelled
as Neo-Dada.

PAIRING UP

Shortly afterwards, Rauschenberg moved to New York City and in 1950 married a fellow student he had met in Paris, Susan Weil; the couple had a child a year later. They were divorced by 1953. Following his marriage, Rauschenberg only had relationships with other men, including, famously, Jasper Johns, another leading light in modern art.

PERFORMANCE ART

Rauschenberg continued to work with Cunningham and other choreographers, designing sets and costumes. He began collaborations with printmakers too, and his popularity grew. In 1964 he was awarded the Grand Prize at the Venice Biennale, the first time the award had been given to an American artist.

ESTATE

BY ROBERT RAUSCHENBERG, 1963

Location: Philadelphia Museum of Art

This large piece was created using a silkscreen process as well as painting and collage. It demonstrates the link between Abstract Expressionism and Pop Art, with sections of Rauschenberg's own photographs, painted splashes of colour and found-media images.

BOB & JASPER

Rauschenberg's "combines" were neither painting nor sculpture; a mixture of both and many of his pieces used found objects and working electrical items, for example.

Rauschenberg was openly gay, and had a long relationship with Jasper Johns. Although homosexuality was not illegal in the USA, it was not widely acceptable in many social circle, before the Stonewall protests in New York in 1969.

"Stuffed cocks and
bound pillows and
fabric sacks that
do double duty
as stand-ins for
butt cheeks and
scrotums."

ARTIST DAVID SPIHER, CRITICIZING AN
EXHIBITION THAT MADE NO MENTION OF
RAUSCHENBERG'S SEXUALITY, 2006

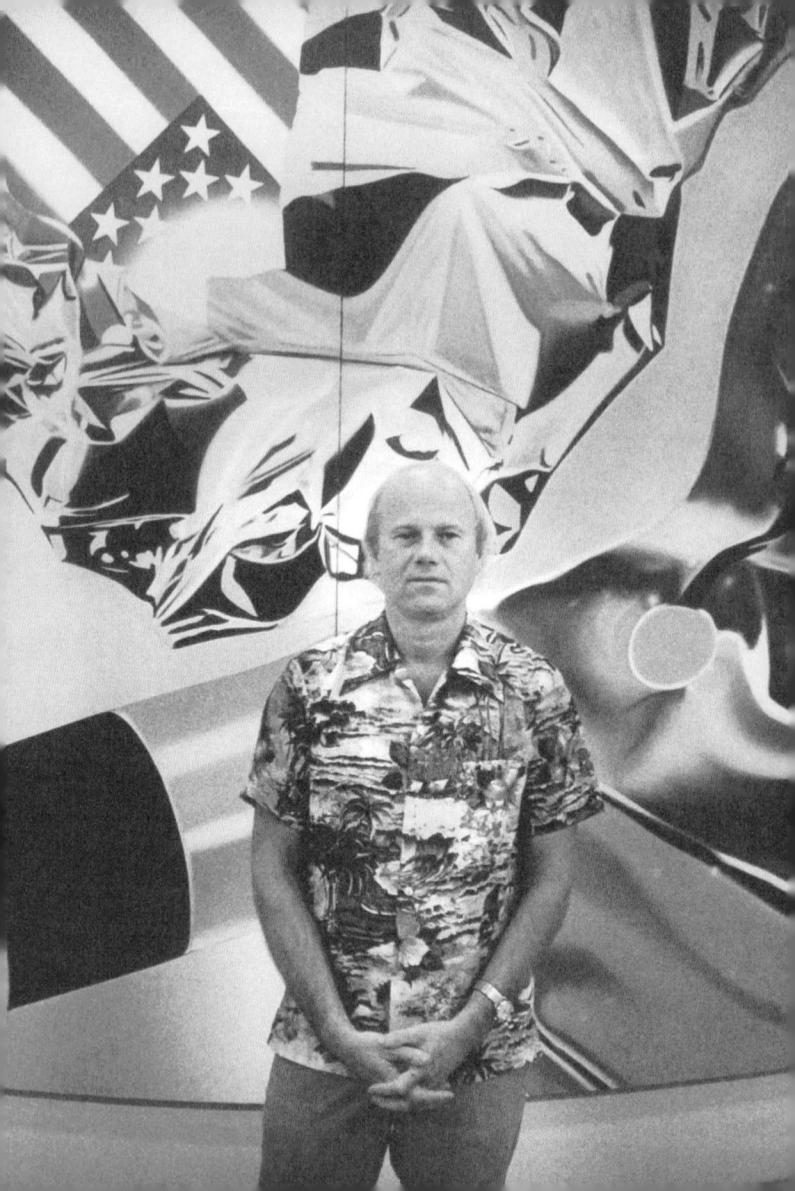

JAMES ROSENQUIST

1933–2017

Place of birth/death:

Grand Forks, North Dakota, USA/
New York, NY, USA

Key works:

President Elect (1960–61)
Marilyn Monroe, I (1962)
F-111 (1964–65)

EARLY YEARS

Unlike the vast majority other artists in Pop Art, James Rosenquist was already a professional painter – of billboards. It is his story more than any other Pop artist that makes the clear link between commercial and fine art.

Rosenquist was born in 1933 in Grand Forks, North Dakota. His family was of Swedish descent. His mother was an amateur painter and the young Rosenquist, in eighth grade, won a scholarship for a short course of lessons at the Minneapolis School of Art.

FAMILY SUPPORT

As a child, Rosenquist was supported in his artistic endeavours by his mother in particular. He would use old wallpaper rolls to draw on as art paper was expensive. Rosenquist attended the University of Minnesota from 1952, where he studied art under the American Abstract Expressionist painter Cameron Booth. In breaks from study, Rosenquist worked as a sign painter.

"I was like a young bum. I had no money. I lived really poorly. I walked everywhere."

JAMES ROSENQUIST,
PAINTING BELOW ZERO: NOTES ON A LIFE IN ART, 2009

MOVE TO NYC

In 1955 Rosenquist moved to New York City and studied at the Art Students League, where his tutors included German surrealist painter George Grosz. He continued his work painting billboards to earn a living.

Rosenquist married in 1960 and moved into new studio space, having quit his job to concentrate on his art full-time. His new pieces tended to be huge, colourful and often political. The best example of this is the enormous, overtly political and critical *F-111* (1965), a comment on American politics and consumerism.

F-111

BY JAMES ROSENQUIST, 1964–65

Location: MoMA, New York, USA

This huge painting measures 10 x 86 feet (3 x 26 metres) and stretches across 23 sections of oil paint on canvas and aluminium. The bright colours and advertisements mix with political images and blend with everyday objects; it all adorns a life-sized US Air Force fighter jet. It is one of the most stunning pieces of contemporary art in the world.

"Generally there's no politics in Rosenquist's fantasies of desire, but in 1965 he produced an exception to that, an enormous panorama about Vietnam."

ART CRITIC ROBERT HUGHES, *AMERICAN VISIONS*, 1997

"Rosenquist is one of the few former pop artists whose work continues unabatedly to have something to say, however elliptic the mode of saying it turns out to be."

ROBERT HUGHES, *TIME*, 1986

ENDURING ART

In later years Rosenquist painted large images and murals all over the world, but worked mainly from his studio in Florida. In 2009, a fire broke out, destroying many of Rosenquist's pieces. The artist died in 2017, at the age of 83, in New York. His work is exhibited all over the world to this day.

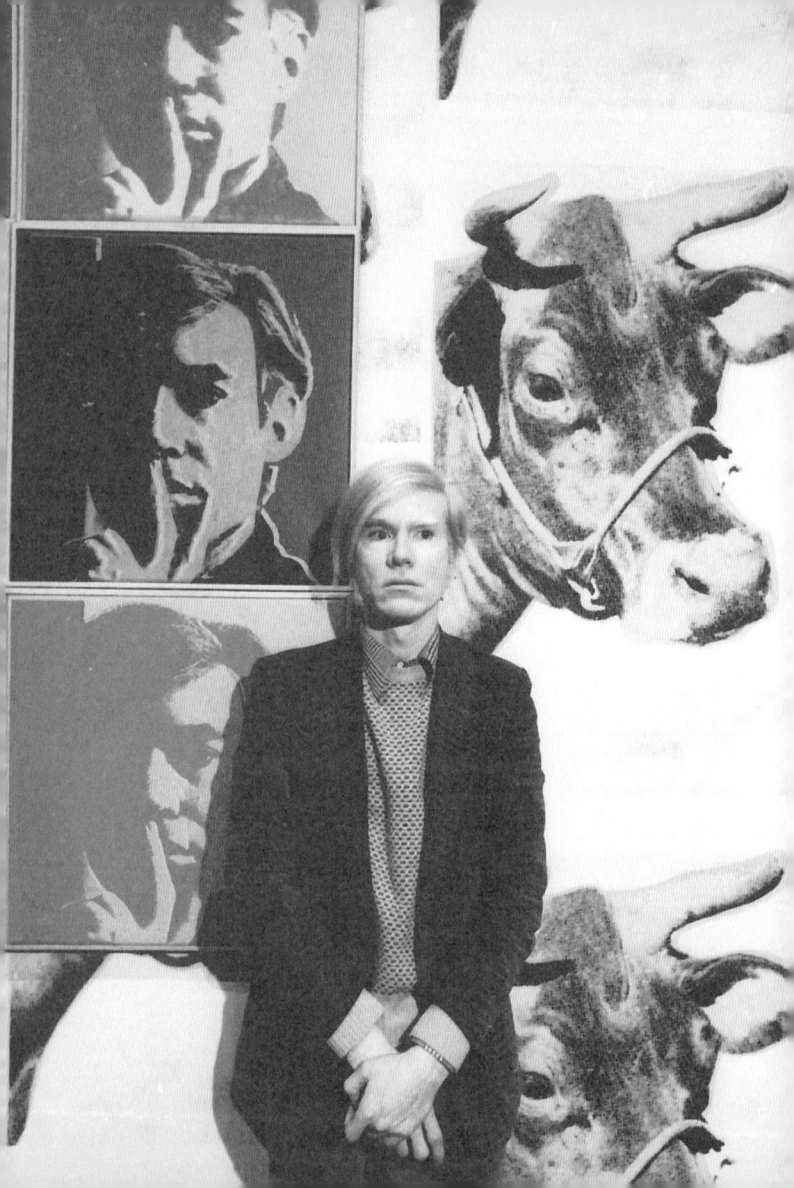

ANDY WARHOL

1928–1987

Place of birth/death:

Pittsburgh, Pennsylvania, USA/
New York, NY, USA

Key works:

Marilyn Diptych (1962)
Campbell's Soup Cans (1961–62)
Banana (1966)
Mao (1972–73)
Self-Portrait with Fright Wig (1986)

WHAT WAS WARHOL?

Andy Warhol is probably the most famous Pop artist of all, and certainly the one with the best-known artwork. His high-colour screen-print style is immediately recognizable and has influenced every subsequent generation of popular artists. He was at the centre of the fascinating mixing of art, fashion, music and celebrity that shaped popular culture in the USA and beyond in the 1960s.

EARLY YEARS

Born Andrew Warhola Jr. in Pittsburgh between the wars, Warhol's parents were immigrants from Austria-Hungary (part of what is now Slovakia). Both worked in a coal mine and Andy was their fourth child. He was a sickly youth, frequently laid low with a various illnesses. His father died when he was 13.

EARLY INFLUENCE

While bedridden, Warhol would listen to the radio for hours, and read movie star magazines. After high school, he attended Carnegie Institute of Technology (now Carnegie Mellon University) in Pittsburgh, studying commercial art.

Warhol graduated in 1949 and moved to New York City, which saw the start of his career as a magazine artist. He also worked as a designer in the shoe industry.

"America started
the tradition where
the richest consumers
buy essentially the
same things as
the poorest."

ANDY WARHOL,
THE PHILOSOPHY OF ANDY WARHOL, 1975

STARTING OUT

Finessing his design and illustrative skills, Warhol started working for RCA Records, designing promotional material and album covers. By 1960 he had his own design studio in Carnegie Hill where he lived. It was during that decade that he learned the screen-printing techniques that he would become so famous for later.

THE FACTORY

By the time Warhol was featured in *Time* magazine in 1962, he – and his work – were gathering interest from collectors and journalists alike. Later that year, his exhibition at the Stable Gallery in New York included some of his classic works, including *Marilyn Diptych*, *100 Soup Cans* and *100 Coke Bottles*. By late 1963 he had opened a new studio, the Factory, which turned into a hangout for musicians, writers and artists.

CELEBRITY CULTURE

Warhol frequently and famously used celebrities (Marilyn Monroe, Elvis Presley, John Wayne) in his work, and became hugely famous as an artist during his lifetime. In many ways he was the purest "Pop artist", mixing with musicians and actors at glamorous parties. He even managed the seminal band the Velvet Underground.

FRIENDS & FILMING

In 1965, Warhol made the announcement that he was to concentrate on film, and cease art production. Many of the people who hung out at the Factory were involved in Warhol's films, including his favoured counter-culture celebrities such as Nico, Joe Dallesandro, Ultra Violet, Jackie Curtis and Candy Darling. Many of Warhol's movies were explicit and it was common for the police to conduct raids and interrupt filming.

ASSASSINATION ATTEMPT

In 1968 Andy Warhol was shot by Valerie Solanas at the Factory. She had appeared in one of his movies the previous year and was the author of the *SCUM Manifesto* (Society For Cutting up Men). Warhol survived but was in hospital for two months.

"Before I was shot,
I always thought
that I was more half-
there than all-there
– I always suspected
that I was watching
TV instead of
living life."

ANDY WARHOL,
THE PHILOSOPHY OF ANDY WARHOL, 1975

Warhol sold his collection of 32 paintings of Campbell's soup cans at his first exhibition in 1962 for $1,000. When they were acquired by MoMA in 1996, they were valued at $15 million.

MARILYN DIPTYCH

BY ANDY WARHOL, 1962

Location: Tate, London, England

One of the most well-known works of art by one of the most famous artists of all time, this piece has everything Pop Art stood for: mass-produced, colourful, meaningful, a doctored appropriated image of a celebrity's image of a celebrity. The original was a publicity shot from the movie *Niagara*, and the piece was finished just weeks after the movie star's death.

1970S & 1980S

Throughout the 1970s, Warhol produced portraits of many more celebrities and famous people, including John Lennon, Diana Ross, the Shah of Iran, Mick Jagger and Brigitte Bardot. Many of these were gathered in the exhibition Andy Warhol: Portraits of the '70s at the Whitney Museum of American Art, 1979–80. It was described by critic Priscilla Tucker as a celebration of "the very commercial celebrity of the '70s".

More than any artist before, Warhol was acutely aware of his worth, and the commercial value of art. He was provocative, challenging and thought-provoking. He was a world removed from the fine artists who preceded him, but his legacy will live on as long as theirs; Warhol will be remembered as one of the greatest artists of all time.

Andy Warhol was one of the artists commissioned for artwork for the Sarajevo Winter Olympics in 1984, alongside David Hockney and others. His speed skater piece was on the event's official poster.

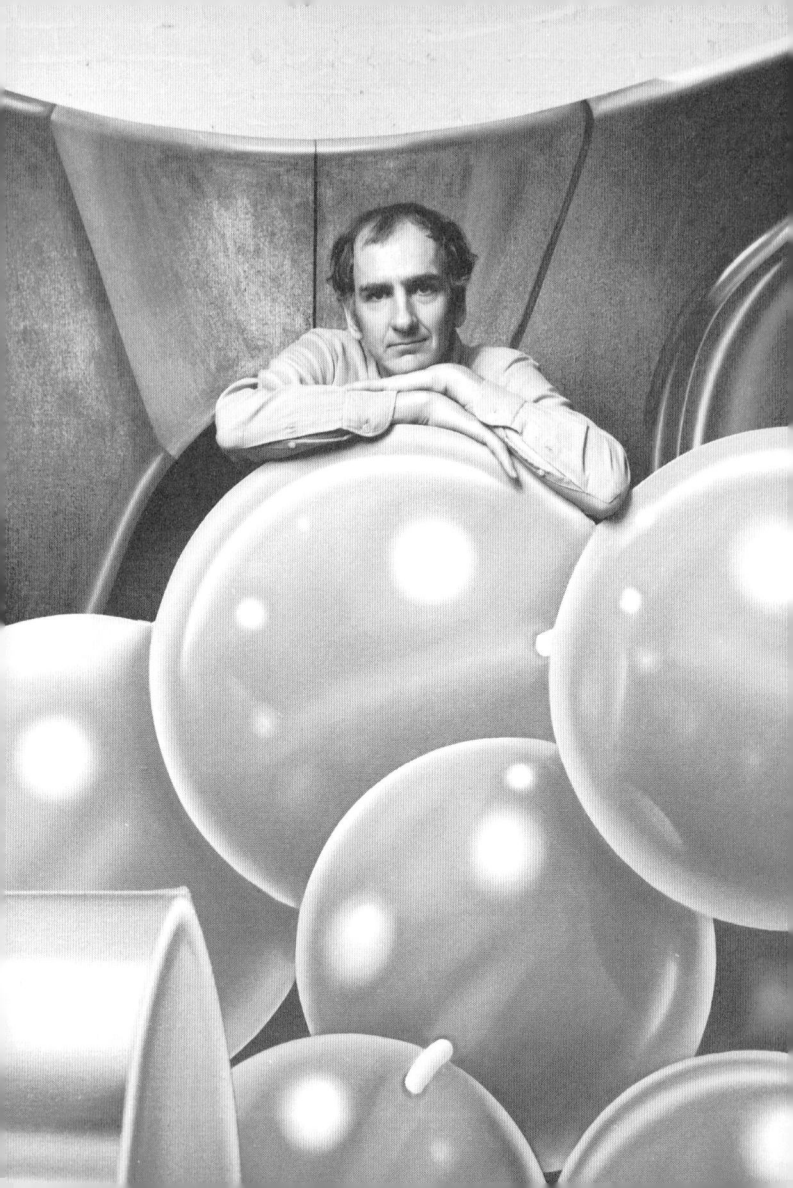

TOM WESSELMANN

1931–2004

Place of birth/death:

Cincinnati, Ohio, USA/New York, NY, USA

Key works:

Great American Nude #21 (1961)
Still Life #35 (1963)
Smoker, 1 (Mouth, 12) (1967)
Monica Sitting with Mondrian (1988)

EARLY YEARS

Tom Wesselmann was born in Cincinnati, Ohio in 1931. Little is known of his early years, but he did later state: "Cincinnati was a negative influence on me as far as art is concerned."

Wesselmann served in the army after two years at college, where he studied psychology. He did not take up fine art immediately, as he wanted to be a cartoonist.

He moved to New York City in 1956 and attended Cooper Union, a highly competitive art school. He became aware of the work of the artist Willem de Kooning (1904–97) and decided to pursue a career as a fine artist.

GOING SOLO

By 1961, Wesselmann mounted his first solo exhibition, and he was part of a loose circle of artists in New York at that time which included Claes Oldenburg and Jim Dine.

His large-format images in series, *Still Life* and *Great American Nude* became very popular, and – whether he liked it or not – he fitted well into the Pop Art movement.

NOT POP ART

Although a part of the art and social scene in New York City that became known as Pop Art, Wesselmann did not really see himself as part of the movement: "At no point do I remember talking art with any of them."

He felt his ideas and imagery differentiated him from it. He felt his work was not as political, and did not offer a critique of consumerism or society in the same way as other Pop artists.

"I dislike labels in general and 'Pop' in particular, especially because it overemphasizes the material used. There does seem to be a tendency to use similar materials and images, but the different ways they are used denies any kind of group intention."

TOM WESSELMANN, *ART NEWS*, 1964

PROGRESSION

Wesselmann continued to paint and create in his series throughout the 1960s and 1970s, adding the famous *Mouth* and *Bedroom Painting* images to his oeuvre.

Wesselmann's *Still Life #20* (1962), for example, features multiple advertising images, a three-dimensional tap, images of food (bananas, sliced bread, Coca-Cola), a cupboard that opens and reproductions of paintings by other artists. *Still Life #28* featured a working television.

STYLE

Wesselmann's works feature bright colours, collage and clear lines, and everyday objects. This makes him as a very important contributor to the Pop Art pantheon, with a style distinct from other artists by his use of sensuality and representations of the role of women in contemporary American society.

"Painting, sex
and humour
are the most
important things
in my life."

TOM WESSELMANN,
INTERVIEW WITH IRVING SANDLER, 1984

BEDROOM TIT BOX

BY TOM WESSELMANN, 1968–1970

An important statement about life, objectification and society, this late-era Pop Art sculpture is fascinating. It features the strong colours and clear lines that demonstrate the link with its artistic predecessors and the rest of the Pop Art movement. Wassermann produced many still life pieces, as well as paintings and sculptures.

FINAL YEARS

By the 1980s, Wesselmann began to work on metal, in particular steel and aluminium. His series of *Steel Drawings* highlights the new skills he employed.

Wesselmann died at the age of 73 following heart surgery. He was married to his wife Claire Selley – a fellow student from Cooper Union – for more than 40 years, and she was a frequent subject of his paintings and sculptures.

"Making money is art and working is art and good business is the best art."

ANDY WARHOL,
THE PHILOSOPHY OF ANDY WARHOL, 1975

"That focus on the sexual revolution of the 1960s is a very important part of his oeuvre... Something about Wesselmann still feels classic."

RACHAEL WHITE YOUNG, CHRISTIES.COM, 2020